THE LITERARY T

A guide to research

George Watson

The literary thesis

A guide to research

Longman

LONGMAN GROUP LIMITED
London
*Associated companies, branches and representatives
throughout the world*

© George Watson 1970

First published 1970

ISBN 0 582 12787 4 (cased)
ISBN 0 582 12788 2 (paper)

Set in 12 point Monotype Bembo
and printed in Great Britain by
The Camelot Press Ltd, London and Southampton

Advance in knowledge is essentially distinction, not aggregation. Each new particular of knowledge is not an addition to, but a newly observed part of, a previously conceived whole.

JOHN GROTE,
Exploratio Philosophica
II, 299

Contents

Part Two   Aids to research

Preface

This advice is offered by a literary historian to those who practise the same art, or who hope to practise it. As a series of hints based on individual observation it naturally has no official standing, and the views I have expressed here commit no one but myself. My chief impulse has been direct experience in British and American universities with the trials of research, both my own and others; and I have been especially stimulated by an annual graduate seminar on research methods which, in the company of several colleagues, I have given for more than ten years in the Faculty of English at Cambridge.

It is sometimes assumed that the transition from the life of the intelligent and industrious undergraduate to that of a graduate student is a natural and easy one. The present account assumes nothing of the kind. In practice research often seems to be fraught with dangers utterly unsuspected by the graduate beginner, and one of my chief objects here has been to encourage him to take stock of these dangers before he begins, or soon after he begins. Research is emphatically not a safe activity, in the sense that undergraduate studies are safe. Intelligent and dedicated students have been known to fail at it. Universities, on the whole, no longer take a sink-or-swim view of the graduate predicament, and will help where help is possible. But the graduate still needs to be told at an early stage that, in the nature of things, there can be no guarantee of fulfilment, and that success may depend on luck as well as virtue. If his ardour is cooled by arguments as well intentioned as these, he may cheer himself with the reflection of having been saved from an existence which might have called for a greater hardihood of mind and capacity for solitude than he could easily claim.

My thanks are due to colleagues in the Cambridge English Faculty who have taught me so much in seminars, and especially to Professor M. C. Bradbrook and Professor Graham Hough. And my intellectual debts to the many graduate students from continental, Commonwealth and American universities, as well as British, who attended the seminar could hardly be greater—and especially to those who spoke up and shared their problems with the rest. Dr R. A. Leigh, Reader in French in the University of Cambridge, and Mr J. C. Maxwell, Reader in English in the University of Oxford, both offered helpful comments on an early draft; and Professor Jonas A. Barish of the University of California, Berkeley, advised me on differences between the British and American systems. Mr A. N. L. Munby, Librarian of King's College, Cambridge, commented at an early stage on the chapter on manuscripts, and Dr J. R. Northam, as Secretary to the Degree Committee of the Cambridge English Faculty, on the intricacies of application procedures; while Professor Morton W. Bloomfield, Chairman of the English Department at Harvard, generously sent me information concerning similar procedures in the United States. And once again Mrs P. Parsons deciphered my hand and typed the whole.

Acknowledgements to authors and publishers for permission to reprint essays at the end of the volume are recorded on page 188, and full details of sources are given under the individual items.

G. W.

St John's College, Cambridge
September 1969

Part One

Preparing a thesis

1. The academic profession

The motive is not in doubt: the principal reason, in practice, to undertake literary research for a higher degree is an ambition to become a university teacher—or, at least, a teacher in a branch of higher education. This ambition is usually based upon undergraduate experience, which is often incomplete; it may arise, indeed, from an acquaintance with no more than two or three academics and a folklore of student conversation. And such folklore sometimes bears only a slight and partial relation to the realities that academics know.

Some realities, fortunately, are familiar and need no emphasis. It is widely understood, in all probability, that the academic is the lowest paid of the higher professions, and that a university career naturally tempts the dedicated rather than the worldly. No man ever became rich through working in a university. Equally, it may be familiar that academics are busy men, and the undergraduate who watches the comings and goings of students at the door of his tutor, supervisor or instructor is unlikely to remain under any other impression for long. The pile of papers and proofs on the desk, too, will tell their own story, and only the most unobservant will suppose that academics work only, or even mainly, in term. The myth of the cloistered calm enjoyed by academics is still powerful outside universities: those inside them quickly learn that it is no more than a myth. A young graduate is far more likely to be attracted to the academic profession because of its opportunities to put his energies to creative use than out of any inclination for repose. Scholarship and teaching both require physical stamina and reserves of nervous energy beyond the ordinary. This is something that even a freshman knows.

Other misconceptions are more widespread, and relate to the vexed and often mysterious question of entrance into the profession. How, in general, is that entrance achieved?

2. Qualifications

It is widely believed that a first-class degree and a postgraduate qualification, especially a doctorate, are both required for admission into the academic profession. Both views are much exaggerated, at least in regard to British universities, though American institutions often lay a firmer emphasis on formal qualifications such as the Ph.D.

The Robbins Report on Higher Education (1963) showed that 41 per cent of university teachers in Britain were without first-class degrees (Appendix 3, para. 45); and that among university teachers appointed in Britain in 1959–61, only 39 per cent held a higher degree at the time of appointment. Only 28 per cent held doctorates (para. 54). Of the 72 per cent appointed without doctorates, some may later have acquired them. But many, too, must have been appointed over the heads of candidates who already held such degrees. It is not at all unusual in appointments in British universities for a candidate without a doctorate to be preferred to a candidate who has one, and there are whole departments or faculties in notable universities in which most members lack the Ph.D.

The tendency towards formal qualifications, none the less, is marked even in the arts, and is readily observable in the fact that younger colleagues are now more likely to possess the title of Doctor than older ones. But this probably represents not so much a policy on the part of those who appoint as a change in the behaviour of students themselves. Graduate programmes, which in Britain are of more recent foundation than on the Continent or in the United States, rapidly create their own momentum. They represent, almost as soon as set in motion, a visible symbol of what the aspiring student supposes to be required of him. They are seen as the ladder by which the beginner must climb. He rarely pauses to notice that many university teachers have not climbed that ladder at all. Some enter the profession shortly after taking their first degree. Others may have preferred or been obliged to achieve an early distinction through publication in a period of sheer poverty or, alternatively, in an employment which allowed some leisure for scholarship. Cases like these, though dwindling, are far commoner than the student can easily guess. It is widely but erroneously assumed that most academics have never been anything but that. The formation of graduate schools, valuable as they often are, has sometimes had the regrettable effect of professionalizing scholarship and reducing the status and function of the private scholar to a point where many now find it impossible to imagine what such a scholar might be like.

It is salutary in this connection to recall that much, and perhaps most, of the literary scholarship for which one is grateful was written by somebody other than a research graduate: by some lonely scholar beyond the range of academic promotion, for instance, or by a busy breadwinner in his spare time. Nobody should feel that careers like these are in their nature inferior to life in a graduate school, and it is not necessarily an advantage to research that it should be undistracted. 'Motives by excess reverse their very nature,' as Coleridge once put it, 'and instead of exciting, stun and stupefy the mind.'[1] Research is not always the better for being full-time. On the contrary, it may 'stun and stupefy' by the deadening predominance it exercises over the mind of a youthful scholar. If the aspirant can delimit his task in a practical way and dispatch it with efficiency, this predominance can be a positive advantage. A graduate has time to work and to

[1] *Biographia Literaria* (1817), ch. xi.

think. Confidence rises, and with good reason, at the sight of work well done. But delay can produce an opposite effect: it can destroy confidence at a premature stage by convincing the unready student, sometimes without sufficient reason, that he lacks all talent for intellectual inquiry.

If the doctorate is one among a variety of possible qualifications for the academic profession, and no more than that, it is also true that there is now more than one road to the doctorate. The Doctor of Letters is usually reserved for senior scholars of international distinction on the evidence of publication; but, in addition, Cambridge University in 1966 instituted a Ph.D. by publication for its own graduates on the evidence of 'proof of a significant contribution to scholarship', and other universities offer, or may soon offer, similar opportunities. It has never been necessary to feel that exclusion from a doctoral programme meant exclusion from scholarship itself; what is more, it need not now mean exclusion even from the doctorate. The life of the graduate student sometimes provides genuine opportunities which individuals of marked originality and exceptional stamina and self-discipline in early adulthood can profit from. But it is an opportunity, not a requirement. Nobody needs the permission of a university to do literary research; and universities themselves, though they may sometimes appear to the new graduate as the sole repositories of human wisdom, do not themselves seek to monopolize the approaches to knowledge.

In the end, there is only one good reason to write a thesis. And that is the ambition to write a good one.

3. The thesis subject

Some university faculties and departments admit graduate students largely on evidence of personal qualification, and defer the definition of subject in the first instance. Others, including the English Faculty at Cambridge, demand a written proposal for research as evidence of personal fitness. This is part of their admission procedure, and is not meant to imply that the proposed subject is immutable. But it provides an admirable opportunity to gauge the ability of an applicant in marshalling an argument, and it helps a committee to judge how suitable its own university may be, in terms of finding a supervisor and providing library facilities, to sponsor such an undertaking. If it causes some aspirants to pause before making an application, this too may be an advantage. An immediate shift from undergraduate to graduate studies is not always a happy one. A conviction which leads to one, two or three years of full-time study and composition needs to be deep and settled, and a proposal ought not to be offered in a merely experimental or provisional mood.

The manner of choice may require some explanation. It is usually a mistake to ask a senior scholar for a subject of research. Many academics have schooled themselves, as a matter of principle, not to answer questions in a form as open as this, though they are usually ready to advise on specific proposals. They are vividly aware that an inclination to research so rootless that it could accept the suggestion of another is unlikely to persist to a successful end. In some continental countries matters are differently ordered, and graduates may even be required to accept a subject suggested by a professor. British universities, however, do not behave in this way.

Many academics have observed that there are broadly two kinds of application to graduate work. In the more numerous and less distinguished category, the application arises from a general inclination to continue the life of a student, and the proposal, which is often couched in a style of affected enthusiasm, is an invention by the applicant which is designed to disguise that inclination. In the second and rarer category, which the graduate programmes of universities exist to welcome and to serve, the application arises from an authentic ambition to answer a significant question of literary history which existing publications do not answer, or to right a wrong—whether a wrongful neglect, or false emphasis, or sheer misunderstanding. These are the genuine applications. They are often made by youthful scholars who, if they could find no place in a university, would settle near some great library and do the work in their own leisure. In cases such as these, universities are eager to sponsor and to help. But those who are responsible for admission are increasingly aware that most applications to research in a university are not of this kind.

Even if the application is genuine, the applicant may labour under certain honest misapprehensions:

1. He may believe, often out of modesty, that his own discoveries are too small to count for much. He may even believe, as a general proposition, that all the larger questions have already been answered or 'done'. A beginner is often excessively impressed by the number of books and articles he has not read, and excessively depressed by the triviality of some that he has read; and he may easily jump to the conclusion that the triviality of some publications points to a state of exhaustion in his subject. This is not so, though the difficulty of dissuading him remains a perfectly real one: it is the difficulty of predicting knowledge which we do not already possess. It is a pity, none the less, when

out of modesty or mistaken conviction a graduate refuses to see the larger significances of what he proposes to investigate.

2. He may, by contrast, exaggerate the value of what he proposes to do. Oddly enough, this can easily arise out of a similar modesty or lack of conviction. An applicant who begins from the mistaken certainty that all the best subjects are already done may also feel, and for just this reason, that he is bound to choose a trivial subject and to cry it up.

3. He may insist on a subject perilously close to his own preoccupations of a doctrinal or even emotional kind. This is a danger to which literary studies are especially, though not uniquely, exposed. It is often claimed that the study of literature bears directly upon the emotional life of the student to a degree unique in academic experience; but it is less often noticed that this can make for a dangerous, even tragic over-commitment as well as for opportunities in self-education. Many unfinished projects of research are of this sort. A successful doctoral project, like any other human activity, needs an element of healthy routine, and the student needs to feel that his plans are moving forward even when he is not in a mood of total commitment. A subject that allows one to live only on the heights is a doomed subject: all the more so if it depends on an intellectual fashion so transient that it may have expired before the work is finished.

When all this is said, it remains true that the commonest failures in proposals for literary research are the polar errors of cosmic vagueness on the one hand and triviality on the other. It may take long and considered reflection to achieve the proper intermediacy of a doctoral proposal: one not too vague, abstract or merely fashionable to attract the justifiable scepticism of an experienced scholar, and yet not so slight as to excite his contempt. It is not an easy compromise to hit. But of the two errors, triviality is surely the graver, since it is less readily open to correction as the work proceeds. A student with an excessively ambitious subject may deliberately and avowedly limit his treatment to certain major aspects: an entirely legitimate and recommended procedure, provided only that he explains what he is about. But a trivial subject cannot be inflated without loss of integrity.

The preface to a thesis, which is most conveniently written last, often serves a useful double purpose of acknowledging debts to those who have helped, other than the supervisor, and of describing, in greater detail than a title-page allows, the precise limits of the investigation and the reasons for special emphasis and notable omissions. In such a matter as this, one can hardly be too blunt and too obvious, and it is a mistake to suppose that what is clear to the author will be equally clear to the reader or examiner. A thesis on Shakespeare's idea of kingship, for instance, which deals with the tragedies rather than the history plays may seem an inexcusable oddity unless it is established at the beginning that the author is guided by some special consideration: that the histories have for this purpose been fully explored already, for instance, and the tragedies not. A thesis entitled 'The Criticism of Matthew Arnold and its Contemporary Relations' which reviews connections stretching from Coleridge to T. S. Eliot ought to make clear, and at the earliest possible stage, that the word 'contemporary' is employed here in an unusual sense. In some cases, where the extent of the subject is a matter of greater complexity than here, it may be a principal part of the function of the first chapter to explain and justify the scope of the thesis, both with regard to what it will include and what it will not. In most cases, however, a plain indication in the preface will suffice.

Changes in direction are common in any form of authorship, and are not in themselves reasons for anxiety. It is usual, after months of work, to discover that some aspects of the chosen subject are more promising than had first been supposed, and others less so. Such changes are often mere shifts in emphasis, and may require no special permission; and this constitutes a reason for offering a title which is not excessively restrictive. The supervisor or adviser will advise whether such shifts are more hopeful than the original proposal and, if so, whether they are so radical as to require official notice. A total change of subject, which sometimes occurs as a possibility when unexpected material suddenly comes to light, will inevitably require such permission.

The regulations of universities concerning reasearch subjects are sometimes less restrictive than is commonly imagined. Cambridge, for example, requires of graduate students a 'dissertation in English embodying the results of their research', and some faculties are ready to interpret this provision widely, being in principle open to proposals for a group of essays as well as for single treatises. The predominant position of the single treatise more usually arises from the ambition of the student to make his mark in a field where he can in a few years achieve total mastery rather than from any restrictive intention on the part of universities themselves. It is difficult enough to become an expert in one subject in two or three years: to become an expert in several may seem to the beginner an even graver challenge. Those universities which allow or encourage a group of essays rather than a single treatise need not much fear a rush of applicants or a lowering of standards.

4. The neglected fields

Some subjects are unpromising because already over-cultivated: the meaning of *Hamlet*, for instance, the dramatic art of Racine or the ethical sensibility of George Eliot. Others are unpromising because, being fashionable, they are now in process of intensive cultivation. It may be useful, then, to consider the tyranny of literary fashion and consider how its perils are best avoided.

It is a significant aspect of the spirit of an age to place a special value upon the arts of a certain historical period. The 1920s and 1930s in the English-speaking world, in a mood of anti-Victorianism, placed a special value upon the English Augustan age; the 1950s and 1960s have since transferred their admiration heavily towards the Victorians, and especially towards their fiction and social criticism. Other ages, such as the Restoration or the later eighteenth century, have never undergone a period of academic vogue, and there is a strong presumption of honesty in favour of those who elect to study them. Nobody, it is true, ought to choose a subject principally out of motives such as those of following or avoiding a fashion. But equally, it should be widely recognized that fashionable interests are in the nature of things exceptionally vulnerable. They are less likely than others to impress as proposals; and they are less likely than others to give rise to an original contribution to the subject. They are perilous in a special sense. It may be difficult, especially for a young graduate, to escape the dominance of the *Zeitgeist* altogether; but he should at least take note of the danger, recognize that much of what he thinks important now may be due to the influence of a department or faculty in which he has studied, of an individual teacher, or of his contemporaries as students. It is no disgrace to take part in the prevailing intellectual atmosphere or in its current of debate. But such currents move fast, and research ought to retain some value for a period of something more than weeks and months. Difficult as it is, the student ought to try to step outside his proposed subject for an instant, to view its weaknesses as well as its strengths, and to ask himself not only 'What at the moment interests me most?' but 'What most needs to be done?'

It is one aspect of the value of an undergraduate training that the graduate may, after some reflection, find himself in a position to answer such a question. He may have heard a specialist remark on a regrettable deficiency in knowledge: 'A pity nobody has ever written a good book on . . .'; or 'Unfortunately this text has never been properly edited.' If the admission is stimulating, the stimulation arises not merely from a mere ambition to fill a gap. There are many subjects which are unprovided because they deserve to be so. But where interests and capacity already exist, a sense of past neglect can properly act as a spur. In some fields it is difficult not to be usefully original. Anybody who offered intelligent critical grounds for extending an interest in Middle English literature beyond the familiar areas of Chaucer, Langland, the *Gawain*-poet and Malory, or who demonstrated revealing connections between fifteenth-century and Tudor intellectual history, or between the Metaphysicals and the age of Dryden, would earn the inevitable gratitude of scholars and students. And so would a student of the Augustan age who could add a comparative dimension to that study by reviewing some aspect of the period in relation to the European Enlightenment, or in relation to new and pertinent historical information concerning the social history of the age. And just as most discussion of the social and ethical attitudes of French and English fiction in the nineteenth century suffers from an air of exhaustion, so do attempts to study the language of fiction in that age, or the relations between its political literature and political history, often demonstrate the possibilities of new and original discoveries.

The beginner may need to be persuaded that the existing state of knowledge is more important than himself. But this is because he does not sufficiently understand that his own interests are often a reflection of the state of the subject at that point in its evolution at which his training happened to occur. A fashionable author, especially one who deserves to be fashionable, may easily afflict the mind with a deceptive sense of discovery. It takes an unusual honesty to admit, or even to perceive, that one may have read him in the first place only because his name was mentioned by acquaintances loudly and often. The inquiring mind properly insists on knowing what those about him are referring to. But whatever the status of such a motive when considered as reason for reading an author, it has little to do with the objects of literary research. A student reads in order to know what others know already. And in that sense one continues as a student all one's life. But a graduate, as such, reads for a further reason, because he hopes to discover what no one else yet knows.

5. *Application of thought*

To research in a subject is not merely to study it. It is rather to ask and answer questions—questions which have not previously been asked and answered. This is the nub of the difference between the intellectual worlds of the undergraduate and the graduate. A graduate may study too, and so may a professor; and there is a plain sense in which one studies to the end of one's days. But what characterizes research is something else: the capacity to see that a question remains unanswered which is worth answering, and the capacity to seek and find an answer by virtue of individual resourcefulness and perseverance.

It is painfully true that some graduate students fail to understand all this at a sufficiently early stage to avoid disappointment. They may be powerfully aware of their own continuing interest in literature, and wish to go on studying it. The thesis subject may then become a pretext for continuing as a student and, more in hope than in expectation, the terms under which further study is conducted. It is not surprising if projects framed with as little sense of commitment as this often end in vacuity and a sense of self-distaste. To attempt one activity under the guise of another, unless a life of deception is natural to one's temperament, readily leads to a condition of mind both unsettled and unproductive. The beginner may object that he has not yet reached a point in his development at which he can frame a question in precise terms and set out to discover an answer that will bear examination by experts in the field. That is often true. But it represents a reason to pause and reflect rather than a reason for committing oneself in advance to unrewarding labour.

It is not easy, at the beginning of a life of scholarship, to understand what a question is like. Many students are unaware how recently much of what is now regarded as elementary in literary history was discovered by scholars who possessed the energy and presumption to pose and answer questions which no one, often enough, had dared to pose before them. The first virtue of the scholar is audacity. The element of mere chance, though occasionally vital, is easy to overstate in matters of intellectual inquiry: a chance remark, a chance find on a bookstall or in a library, a chance discovery of a cache of papers, are often supposed to be the natural impulse for literary research. Many scholars, out of modesty, love to recount their own careers in these terms. But other men hear chance remarks, or happen upon books or manuscripts, and still fail to recognize the significance of what they hear or see. 'In the field of observation,' as a French scientist once remarked, 'luck favours only the mind that is well prepared.' The following considerations, then, may help to clarify what a question in literary history is like, and how it is best recognized.

1. A question is not a statement. It is not the object of literary research, as it often is of moral philosophy, to remind the reader of what he already knows. If something is known to be the case, then it is not a question. It is known, for example, that the novels of Thomas Hardy were extensively reviewed in England and America. 'The critical reception of Hardy's novels', then, though it may prove a sufficient title for a thesis, is not a question. But certain questions might, in a given state of the subject, be held to arise out of it. Did Hardy pay significant attention to reviews, for instance, and does the evidence for such attention appear in the novels themselves; and if so, what effect upon his novels did such attention have; and how, if at all, do these effects change from one stage to another in his career as a novelist? Dryden, as a dramatist, is known to have been influenced by Hobbes's ideas; or rather,

it is known that Aubrey believed that he was. But it remains a question whether Aubrey had sufficient reason to say so, and whether any of the major differences between Restoration drama on the one hand and Renaissance drama on the other can be accounted for by a shift in philosophical and political preconceptions after the *Leviathan*. It is known that T. S. Eliot radically revised *The Waste Land*, and instructive to study the nature of that revision. But research would require something more than that. What were Eliot's probable motives in revision, and how are they to be estimated in individual instances of cuts and changes; and how do they relate to the doctrines of Eliot's literary acquaintances at that time, and to his own? To assert an interest in a given area of the subject is the merest beginning, and might better be described as a stage that precedes the beginning. The real start to research is marked by a point of interrogation.

2. A question is often well directed against an easy assumption. The student is surrounded by examples of such assumptions, though he may only slowly learn to realize how vulnerable some of them are. The liveliest and bitterest intellectual controversies may often assume a premiss common to both sides. But what, it may be useful to ask, is the evidence for the premiss itself? What reason is there to think that Shakespeare's sonnets are in any sense autobiographical, or indeed that they include historical features of any kind? or that any major author in the Age of Reason believed in the supremacy of reason in the manner which the phrase implies? or that any major Victorian thinker believed in *laissez-faire*? or that the social fiction of England presents sufficient reasons for believing that the class war ever existed? Many theses suffer from a failure to question what desperately needs to be questioned. That certain terms are widely used and widely accepted is not a reason for swallowing them now. A phrase like 'Defoe's bourgeois ethics', for example, may naturally elicit the following questions from an alert examiner: what is the evidence for supposing that there was a bourgeoisie in early eighteenth-century England? or that it possessed a characteristic

ethic of any kind? or that this kind was like Defoe's? Such questions might present a formidable challenge at the last ditch of a thesis. On the other hand, a student who *began* his inquiries by posing questions as radical as these might end with a thesis or a book that proved formidable in itself.

3. Assumptions may be questioned and impaired, or even overturned, by sheer severity of logic; though in literary history such logic will always need to be verified by evidence and buttressed by a reasonable degree of documentation. Certain familiar positions cannot be true, or at least are very unlikely to be true; and something like certainty in such matters may even be glimpsed before one has left one's armchair. Many graduates spend too much of their time in amassing evidence, in the hope that a question will emerge in the course of accumulation. And certainly evidence will have to be gathered at some point: but it is also observable that some truths follow from others in a logical pattern, and that this pattern is sometimes discernible before the evidence has been sought. The simple formula 'If p, then q' epitomizes certain crucial stages in the practice of literary history as in the practice of other intellectual disciplines. If it were true that the New Learning of the sixteenth century was hostile to the creative arts, then certain consequences would follow concerning the works of those humanists who wrote plays and poems; and if they do not follow, then the premiss itself is open to reasonable doubt. If seventeenth-century England really preferred Ben Jonson to Shakespeare as a dramatist, then significant consequences would follow concerning the state of critical opinion in that century; or alternatively, the evidence for supposing Jonson to have been the preferred dramatist may itself be open to question. The movement from p to q could rarely, if ever, be conclusive in itself in a literary question. But it is one of the sure marks of talent in a student to see him ready to argue provisionally in these terms. It is a guarantee both of the lucidity of his mind and of his irreverence for received ideas.

4. A question is aimed at an answer, and at an answer to itself.

It is a matter of plausibility (to put the matter no higher) that the whole thesis, and even its individual chapters, should be shaped in such a way that beginning and end stand in some visible and enlightening relationship to each other. A chapter that begins by posing one question and ends by answering another, even if a better one, fails to carry conviction in its own terms. It is one of the supreme attractions of authorship that one is allowed to set one's own examination papers, so to speak, before attempting to answer them. But 'set' they none the less are, and they need to be answered in the terms offered. The internal solidity of a thesis depends upon a sense of correspondence between what it proposes and what it does.

5. Answers can be surprising, subversive to one's own convictions or (what is often hardest to bear) simply boring. It may be difficult not to flinch in any of these cases, and the temptation to prevaricate, to tamper, or to enliven at the expense of truth may be severe. This is the ultimate test of serious purpose in research. A student whose subject is the rise of the industrial novel in the England of the 1840s, for instance, and who approaches his subject out of an ambition to glorify the role of the masses in the early years of the Industrial Revolution, may find his faith and his poise disturbed by what the novels, the pamphlets and the social history of that time reveal to him. Literature does not always tell us what we want to hear. But to offer to pursue a question to the end is to undertake to accept the findings and to announce them when found. The original question was not, after all, merely a rhetorical one.

6. *The approach*

A programme for research arises most naturally out of a powerful undergraduate interest, such as an enthusiasm for an author or a sense of dissatisfaction with the existing state of a question. The transition is more troublesome than is sometimes hoped, and aspirants need to be warned that it is often subject to greater difficulties of mental adjustment than the transition from school-boy to undergraduate. It is emphatically not to be made either hurriedly or without genuine commitment, and students who embrace research out of a disinclination to attempt anything else often find that they have chosen a role they cannot sustain. Intelligence and a general interest in the subject as a whole, which usually ensure success in an undergraduate career, are necessary but not sufficient talents in a graduate student. He needs a perseverance well beyond the ordinary as well, a talent for self-discipline and an advanced sense of tactical judgement in the choice of a subject. Neither the inclination to continue as a student nor the ambition to become a university teacher will in themselves sustain him through years of strenuous and often solitary labour.

It is as well to estimate the situation at an early stage. Literary research is, among other things, a form of authorship, and authorship is subject to its own characteristic malaise. This may arise from nothing more irrational than a continuous consciousness of oneself as existing in the shadow of examples of literary excellence which one cannot equal. The sentence one is writing could always be better than it is. Those who experience periods of anxiety or sheer unhappiness may be helped by the reflection that this is part of the common lot of the man of letters. It is a task that requires stoicism as well as talent. If it has its characteristic joys, it is realistic to expect that they should come late rather than soon, and only from the knowledge of work well done.

In approaching the design and ordering of a thesis, it is a practical necessity to spy out the land in advance. To propose a major author as a subject, for instance, could only carry conviction if based on an existing knowledge of the material. Not to have read widely in that author—and not to have read, or at least read in, the principal secondary works published over the past generation—would suggest a view of research both precipitate and perilous. A proposal made blind is not a serious proposal; if one is to spend one, two or three years in full-time research, it is a practical necessity to ascertain in advance what is involved. To demand this is to demand an outline, and no more than that. But the outline needs to be there if the proposal is to be regarded in a serious light. The adviser or supervisor, certainly, will be impressed at the first meeting in direct proportion to his sense that the student has already taken grip of his subject in outline: that he knows enough about the scholarly state of the subject, for instance, to know which aspects are well provided for and which neglected, which the unrewarding ones and which the points of growth. And to know that is to have read at least the most recent works in the subject, even if later inquiry proves that they are not the best.

Borderline or interdisciplinary subjects are especially open to this requirement. A subject which relates literature to some bordering discipline such as social or political history, musicology, philosophy, iconography or linguistics may have its unique attraction: the prospect of achieving a strikingly original discovery, it is often hoped, through importing into literary studies the findings of other disciplines. But the need to look before leaping is even greater here than elsewhere. A merely amateur interest in the allied discipline, certainly, will not suffice, and the candidate who ventures from literature into social history, for example, may find a professional social historian among his examiners. This is not to say that he would need himself to become a social historian; but certainly his knowledge in the field would need to amount to something more than a mere smattering. In invading the preserves of another discipline, moreover, it is perilously easy to accept outdated assumptions and to neglect the recent findings of a body of scholarship in which one has no special competence. Subjects like these may be moving as fast as literary studies themselves, and it is prudent to discuss the problem with an expert. A university, after all, is often the ideal setting in which to conduct an interdisciplinary inquiry, since its members are free to avail themselves of the teaching of many departments. Attendance at a class or lecture, or a polite letter to a scholar in the appropriate discipline asking for advice and a meeting, will often find a generous response. But expert advice needs to be taken early— just as soon as the question has been precisely formulated, in fact—to prevent the graver disappointments of following false trails and of finding oneself hopelessly lost.

In any event, it is essential to recall that the academic study of the great literatures of the world is an expanding international activity. It is likely enough that dozens, perhaps even hundreds, of graduates around the world are already at work on one's chosen subject, or on something much like it. To take stock of the situation now is the best way of avoiding disappointment later. It is naïve to suppose that anyone possesses rights of monopoly over any intellectual subject whatever, however publicly he may announce his intention of pursuing it. Disappointment on this score is often misplaced, in any case: unless the subject is more sharply defined than most, it is unlikely that two theses will coincide in substance as well as in title. Uniqueness is a property of mind that anyone, intelligent or not, may reasonably take for granted in himself. Confidence on this score is in any case a necessary qualification for the task—all the more so since it may tend to evaporate in the course of writing.

Much research is disappointing in its immediate results. But then it is nobody's fault if research sometimes means the following of blind alleys and the dismissal of possibilities which once looked promising. Any original intellectual inquiry is as likely to include experiences of this kind as it is to record moments of exhilarating discovery. Time is almost inevitably wasted, if it can be called wasteful to arrive at a negative result; in the early stages of research, especially, it would be surprising if it were otherwise.

A subject needs to bear some relation to the place in which it is proposed to pursue it. If it requires the use of a manuscript, or of some special collection of books, then it is natural to apply to a university within reach of that manuscript or that collection. Universities are more than usually ready to extend hospitality when they recognize their own facilities to be in some sense or other unique; and conversely, they may take the view that a good candidate with a good subject cannot be accepted if he cannot easily pursue that subject on the spot, or near it. The same considerations may apply to advice and supervision. An overseas candidate, for instance, who is anxious to pursue some question relating to the literature of his own country in a British or American university, may often feel that his native experience and language give him a special advantage. But he should also consider whether that advantage can be put to any effect in the university to which he applies. It is useful, in such cases, to inquire first whether a suitable library and other facilities exist: if they do, such information can help to give an air of serious intention to the application when it is made. In admitting candidates, committees often ask not only 'Can he do it?' but also 'Can he do it here?'

And finally, the candidate who offers a subject for research should ask himself the demanding question 'What is it for?' A thesis is not merely an educational procedure: it is also a work intended to impress a scholar in the subject on its own merits. It answers questions that need to be answered; and those answers, if the venture is well conceived and successful, will be used by other scholars in teaching and writing. It is best to confront the issue of purpose at an early stage. A positive answer will help to ensure not only the ultimate success of the thesis but also the confidence of the student as he works.

7. *Editing*

Not all graduate students are fully aware that an edition is in principle as acceptable a subject as any, and that, considered as a thesis subject, it may have clear advantages over a treatise or group of essays. First, it poses no problems or difficulties of purpose, since it is self-evident that many texts need to be edited in order to be understood. A student who edits a literary text other than a trivial one need never doubt that his work will be used or that the future will in some measure be grateful for what he has done. Further, he need not feel under the slightest obligation to accept the second-best. In the modern vernacular literatures, at least, there is no need for the aspiring editor in search of a text to scrape barrels. Many major texts are, in the modern understanding of the term, simply unedited. In English, for instance, this remains true of much late medieval literature, of a good deal of Renaissance literature, especially in the case of prose works such as Hooker's *Laws*, of most Restoration drama and, with certain distinguished exceptions, of neoclassical and romantic literature as well. In the nineteenth and twentieth centuries the situation, naturally enough, is even more open. And it cannot be assumed that works which were once well edited could not usefully be edited again, since the progress of literary history following a major edition often provokes further discoveries. The student may feel that such an undertaking as re-editing smacks too much of mere synthesis or compilation. But he will quickly find that, in collating the discoveries of others, his own findings arise naturally out of the partialities or incompleteness of his predecessors. If an editor does his work with proper application, then it is often positively difficult for him not to contribute to the subject. No edition, in all probability, is so good that it cannot be improved upon, though the student should for just this reason avoid the excesses of self-congratulation that sometimes follow the very natural discovery that a great scholar has made a mistake or two. In addition, the student may welcome the sense of continuity which editing, unlike many kinds of research, confers on him. The element of routine, properly considered, is one of its greatest blessings. At least it is always obvious what the next question to be answered is.

To edit is to prepare a text and write an introduction and commentary. Textual criticism is a fully explored activity, and cannot be discussed here. An introduction may amount to a critical essay of substance, and may be used to guarantee the editor's intelligent concern for the text and his ability to perceive what is at stake there: its historical relations, its permanent intellectual interest, and its status as a work of art. With such an introduction as this, nobody need feel that the editorial art is constrictive. As for the commentary, it is perhaps best to admit at once that few general directives are of use. But no editor who is ready for his task needs to feel himself working in a vacuum. He knows that his audience is a scholarly one, and one that will not thank him for being informed on matters of general knowledge such as who Socrates was, or of facts readily available in familiar works of reference. The reader of a scholarly edition should always be assumed to be more intelligent than oneself. The student will also know an existing edition of a text similar to his own which he can readily use as a model. And in such matters example outstrips precept by a wide margin. The best way to remind oneself how to write an annotation with point and succinctness is to keep an admired commentary at one's side and to imitate its procedures. In a matter as technical as this, originality is of no interest. Those who turn to a scholarly edition expect it to do the work done by other editions which they already know. They will be pointlessly confused by an elaborate and idiosyncratic list of abbreviations, inconsistent punctuation and underlining, or unexplained allusions to unfamiliar works. It is better as well as easier to follow the stream: unless, indeed, some demanding reason which arises out of the work itself forbids it. And if the subject falls naturally within the scope of a publisher's series of scholarly repute, there may be a double reason for using an existing edition as a model. It could provide not merely a ready tool for editorial method but, at some later date, an opportunity for publication too.

8. The scale of the thesis

Universities have excellent reasons for imposing statutory limits on the length of a thesis, and this practice is usually followed by British and American, though not always by continental, universities. As a practical reason, they would find it difficult or impossible to find examiners for a thesis of inordinate length. And the student, too, needs the protection of an assurance that his work will be judged in terms of works of restricted length. He may be aware that his situation is not literally competitive; but he might still be justifiably alarmed to hear that a doctorate in his own university had recently been awarded to a work of hundreds of thousands of words. In any case, his programme is rightly governed by considerations of time, and the plight of the eternal student cannot be recommended on any ground whatever. The statutory word limit, in effect, is a blessing to all concerned. Its precise terms differ somewhat from one university to another: in Cambridge English, for example, there is a limit of 80,000 words for the doctorate and 60,000 for the M.Litt. If the thesis is an edition, then the edited text does not normally count as part of the thesis for this purpose.

Such figures are limits, not targets. There are no marks for length, and a thesis is seldom if ever too short. It is judged on grounds of substance and presentation alone, and the task of concentrating an argument within a limited span of words, avoiding diffuseness and jettisoning support arguments and superfluous evidence, may be among its most educative aspects. Though special permission to exceed the statutory limit may be requested and on occasion granted, students should know that such requests do not inspire confidence in their ability to organize and select material; and that examiners are inclined to look with sour disfavour upon theses which strive to achieve a special advantage through mere bulk. The mastery of an author is seen in what he leaves out. To collect exhaustive evidence is one thing: to dump it inconsiderately into the thesis without selection is another. In most discussions it is entirely proper to summarize an argument in a manner which carries conviction. Only conclusions which are profoundly contrary to established opinion need, on the whole, to be protected by a battery of all the evidence.

9. *Composition*

It is sometimes supposed that literary research consists of a long reading programme accompanied by extensive taking of notes, and ending in a short, sharp burst of composition. This procedure commonly ends in frustration and failure, and for good reason. There is nothing in the literary life as dispiriting as a large pile of notes, even if they are clear and legible. An untidy collection would be enough to terminate any but the sturdiest literary ambition. A graduate student has usually written nothing longer than a weekly essay or term paper, and he can too easily suppose that the life of a graduate means a release from the deadline. He may need powerful persuasion to be convinced that books and theses are written by stages and in sections, and that each stage is best marked by a determination to deliver a unit of the work in something approaching its finished form. Composition best begins early. It is only after one has begun to write, as any author knows, that one begins to understand what the questions really are. And it is only after one has written, in however limited a degree, that the mere aspiration to write is steadied into a controlled and resolute enthusiasm.

The first step is to draft a Table of Contents. If this course sounds impetuous, that can only be on grounds of misunderstanding. The first table is not intended to commit anyone to anything: it exists to clear the student's mind, and the supervisor's, on what is proposed. The completed thesis may bear little or no

relation to it, but it will none the less have fulfilled its proper purpose. It is common, almost universal, to change one's mind, but
one must first have a mind to change. An author wants to surprise
himself; but in order to do so, he must put his first thoughts into
a visible pattern, if only in order to test weaknesses. Until a short
group of provisional chapter titles in provisional order have
appeared in a column on a sheet of paper, it is impossible to ask
the first practical questions of authorship that arise: where one is
to start writing (which may easily prove not to be Chapter 1);
what one will have to read to fill the most manifest gaps in knowledge; where, perhaps, one may need to go for special materials;
and above all, how the task can hopefully be allocated over the
period in view. There is little point in delaying these decisions,
even if they prove optimistic or, in the light of unexpected discoveries, simply mistaken. If the proposal is a genuine one, a
draft table of contents should arise almost irresistibly out of it.

More than that, the insistent problem of design, once solved, is
itself a programme of action. The draft table will usually make
clear on the instant what is immediately possible and what is not.
This is the point at which one begins to write, and it is best to
begin soon: but the draft of the first chapter to be composed can
hardly be attempted unless it already exists in some notional
relationship to the rest. An author needs to know that certain
issues can be omitted here because they will be treated elsewhere:
he cannot afford to try to argue the whole matter at every point.
And a table of contents will give him the security of limitation
that he needs. One can sit down with reasonable confidence to
compose a given Chapter 3 of defined scope: one can hardly
attack the whole. Equally, one can sit down to write a unit of up
to 10,000 words with some confidence of success: one can hardly
sit down with the general intention of writing a thesis or a book.

A table of contents may be a necessary step, too, in the collection of evidence. It is one of the inconveniences of research
that one rarely if ever discovers materials in the order in which
they are to be used. A small loose-leaf notebook, which is for

many purposes more practical than cards, being harder to lose and less susceptible to careless shuffling, may be of use here. If the pressmarks of essential books are recorded there, time will be saved in the library. One procedure is to lay out the notebook with the provisional chapter headings, so that evidence can be entered at once in the appropriate place. Hobbes, when he was writing *Leviathan*, is said to have found it helpful to know in advance what order to confer upon his notes: 'He had drawn the design of the book into chapters,' says Aubrey, 'so he knew whereabout it would come in.' It is not always realized early enough that research requires a high degree of efficiency in the sorting out and storing of evidence. Such efficiency may be through methods peculiar to oneself, and with great scholars it often is; but it needs in some sense or other to be there. And certainly the notion that research requires less efficiency than an executive career is highly unwarranted. An administrator or businessman has a secretary, after all, to be efficient on his behalf: the graduate student commonly does not. If he makes a time-wasting error in efficiency, such as losing a reference, there is no one else who will recover it for him.

Some students find it difficult to write, and they do not always recognize how usual this condition is. Many authors find it difficult to write too; and more especially, difficult to start. Tentative suggestions can be offered in the face of this delicate problem, though hardly in the hope that much that is essential will not be sacrificed to generality. One solution which may appeal to the strong-willed is the solution of pure self-discipline: like Browning's determination, at one point in his career, to write a poem a day. In scholarly terms, this might mean writing at least a page a day; and it might include a determination to sit at one's desk at a given hour. Since the lives of many graduate students are desperately lacking in a sense of fixity, the very precision of this demand could be its principal strength. And it may help to realize how little, in terms of a daily task, a book or thesis requires. Its total bulk may at first intimidate. But a thousand words is not much to write at a sitting, and a mathematical calculation based on this, or any similar proposal, will make that bulk dwindle in the imagination to a matter of months. It is always a good tactic in composition to stop for the day at a point where further progress is easy: in that way, writing can the more readily be resumed.

A further, and perhaps more humane, device may be of more use in certain cases. Some authors find it difficult to write because they can hardly conceive of their audience. They would not encounter the same difficulty in conversing or in writing a letter to an acquaintance. If it seems hard to begin, it may seem easier to cast the first draft in the form of a letter addressed to a supervisor or adviser.

A third suggestion is based on an analysis of how composition ordinarily occurs. With scholarly prose the process is often threefold:

1. the making of notes, which begin to form the pattern of an argument;
2. the first draft; and
3. the revision, in which details are filled in, quotations and references verified and inelegancies of style reduced for the fair copy.

It is at Stage 2 that the gravest difficulties usually occur. Most authors find collecting materials and scribbling notes almost too delightful; so much so, that the real problem may be not how to start but how to stop. And revision is not usually a painful process: once the prose is on the page, in however misshapen a condition, it is usually easy enough to see what needs to be done. If Stage 2 presents the critical problem, then, it may be because not enough of the weight has been shifted to either side. And this problem can be lightened, at least, by determining in advance to distribute some of that weight. A writer who learns early how to take notes in a full and ordered way—at least halfway towards formal prose—and to defer, as he composes his first draft, many of his finer stylistic decisions to a later stage of revision, may soon find that his writing block has dwindled or disappeared.

34

10. Argument

A literary thesis is usually an argument; and if, as is often the case, it concerns an author of reputation, then it is likely to represent a single stage in a long and continuing debate. This is an inevitable aspect of intellectual progress in the arts and sciences, and to protest that such work goes quickly out of date is to miss the point: it is precisely by virtue of going out of date that contributions to human knowledge best serve the purpose for which they were designed. Few students of physics read Sir Isaac Newton now, simply because Newton's discoveries have been exploited and revised by later discoverers. And they were exploited and revised because they were worth it. An intellectual discovery would need to be worthless, in ordinary circumstances, in order to survive in precisely the form in which it was offered.

An argument is in some degree polemical. It is certainly no mere assemblage of facts, though it may choose to assemble facts, at certain points, for certain specific purposes. The commonest reason for writing a thesis, and often the best, is that the student has come to believe that there is something mistaken or inadequate in the existing state of the subject that he wishes to correct. Such dissatisfaction is among the foremost of scholarly impulses. It sharpens the will to work and to write, since the task amounts to one of righting a wrong. And it helps to shape the argument itself, so that evidence coheres in a lucid pattern. When justice is being done, as in a lawyer's summing-up or in a political speech, there is nothing mysterious or vague about the relation between the case presented and the evidence called in its support. The polemical cast is the strongest and most satisfying of all in which to shape and compose a work of scholarship.

It follows that open disagreements with established scholars are well in order. Such disagreements, if well marshalled, may help to build a logically impressive structure as nothing else can do. Only two provisos need to be entered here. The first is that dis-agreement should be courteous, whether the opponent is alive or dead, and should leave in the reader no impression of vindictive pleasure. A scholarly opponent is rarely injured by attacks of this sort: the author himself always is. The other proviso is that the target should be a significant one. A merely absurd view is not worth an answer. A polite duel may help to marshal an argument, but it could only leave an impression of triviality if the opponent is plainly unworthy of the fight. And duels are only useful if a misconception is widespread. There can be no point in taking on Dr X if nobody ever thought him right, and no point in be-labouring errors as trivial as inaccurate quotation or transcription. They may be worth mentioning, but not worth emphasizing. Nobody, in all probability, is altogether immune from these charges, just as no edition is textually impeccable. It is best to practise the charity that one needs.

A sense of damaging isolation is often suffered in authorship, and nowhere more easily than here. The degree to which the arguments of others are worth attacking or ignoring is a matter relative to the intellectual atmosphere in which one lives. Nothing clears the mind so quickly on such matters as a conversation, and not necessarily with an expert. It is always clarifying to be asked what one is doing, and why. Equally, the tone in which scholarly arguments are best conducted may helpfully be exposed to criti-cism as soon as they are written; and again, not necessarily to the criticism of an expert. It may be instantly obvious to an observer that reasonable courtesy has or has not been maintained, that a fact supposed by the author too evident to be worth mentioning is not evident at all, or that a point laboured in a first draft is already so widely accepted that it hardly needs now to be made at length.

11. *The use of evidence*

The first gleam of the scholarly instinct, which may dawn even upon the schoolboy, is that not everything in print is true. The second is that not everything in print is of equal truth. The sure mark of the beginner is to suppose that all published works are of equal dignity, and that he must read them all before he begins to write. Research is a matter of instinct as much as perseverance, and an experienced scholar learns to sense in advance what books and articles will be of use to him, and what parts of those books and articles. Dr Johnson, it is said, was scornful of those who insisted on reading books all the way through. If a book has a table of contents and an index, they are there to save time that will be needed for other books.

It is natural to attempt to take possession of a subject by reading widely in secondary sources. And there are usually efficient guides: the major periods of English literature, for example, all have annual bibliographies devoted to them in American scholarly journals. But it is dampening to draw up a long list of works of modern scholarship with the ambition of reading them through. Reading needs to be more intimately connected with composition than that, more diversified, and more readily subject to creative diversion. In any case, a corpus of scholarly material is not usually best approached in the order in which it was written. One begins more profitably with the most recent publications, working backwards in an increasingly selective pattern. In the case of major authors, where knowledge moves fast, the most recent works will tend to put much previous work out of date and to emphasize, in any case, whatever in older scholarship may still be worthy of remark. And it is natural to expect a recent edition to excel all its predecessors. There are many exceptions: all that is in question here is the assumption from which an aspiring scholar can intelligently begin. It is one of the refinements of expert knowledge to discover, by trial and error, that a certain nineteenth-century biography or edition is better than anything since. That may be well worth knowing and well worth announcing. But it is still natural to uncover exceptions of this sort by starting with the most recent scholarship one can find.

The vital distinction between primary and secondary is sometimes ignored by the beginner. If one is working on Dickens, then the works of Dickens are primary evidence, and what Gissing or George Orwell wrote about them is secondary. A quotation from the one is quite different in status from a quotation from the other. This is not offered in disparagement of an acquaintance with secondary sources, which is plainly a necessity: such acquaintance prevents one from offering with an air of discovery that which is already known, or from asserting with an air of confidence what has already been disproved. Acton once complained of Buckle that 'he has taken great pains to say things that have been said much better before in books he has not read'.[1] There is no avoiding the duty of learning the state of play. But equally, there is no point in thinking it more than an essential precaution. Secondary sources are not similar in value to the works themselves: they cannot be used as bricks in the building, still less as foundation stones. What Gissing or Orwell thought of Dickens, however informed and perceptive, is in the end no more than that. If they were right, there may be some special case for reviewing the evidence in order to show why; and if they were not, their mistake may give a welcome opportunity for casting

[1] *Lord Acton and his Circle*, ed. Abbot Gasquet (London, 1906), p. 13, from a letter of 30 March 1858.

the argument into a fine polemical mould. But these are mere matters of tactic, and the reasons for quoting such sources at all can never be more than formal or rhetorical reasons. In an absolute sense, there are no authorities. In demonstrating, for some special reason, the state of a subject, one may powerfully help to shape one's own argument; but it is only the shape and value of that argument itself that can properly justify the procedure. A thesis is not strictly bound to mention secondary sources at all, though in practice it would be an unusual thesis that failed to mention some. It is simply bound to take account of them—to be composed in such a manner as to make clear that the state of the subject has been well understood. That can certainly be achieved without the dropping of many names; and long digressions or footnotes recounting the history of the question in modern scholarship, though not forbidden, are equally not required.

In many areas of literary studies it is needlessly confining to assume that the only evidence, or even the best, is always to be found in books. In some fields, such as French and English literature in the last two hundred years, periodicals often secrete both original texts and secondary information still unused by modern scholarship. The terrain is still largely unmapped, though Walter E. Houghton, *The Wellesley Index to Victorian Periodicals 1824–1900* (Toronto, 1966–), has begun the enormous task of listing articles in the great Victorian periodicals with author-attributions of anonymous items; the *Index* already includes the *Edinburgh Review* from its foundation in 1802. Daily and weekly papers are more difficult to consult than monthlies and quarterlies, though some are indexed volume by volume: for *The Times*, for instance, there are a number of indexes, including *Palmer's* (1790–1941), and an official index since 1906, now a two-monthly. Because of the change of calendar in England from Old Style to New in September 1752 it may be necessary to adjust the year for pre-1752 dates occurring between 1 January and 24 March.

Information about the locations of periodicals since the seventeenth century in over four hundred British libraries is available in

James D. Stewart, *British Union-Catalogue of Periodicals*, 4 vols (London, 1955–58, with supplements). To consult newspapers it may be necessary to visit the British Museum Newspaper Library at Colindale, London NW9. The prospects for discovery here are exceptionally inviting, especially in the Victorian and modern periods, where many public pronouncements by men of letters remain buried and unnoticed in press reports. If the date of a public speech is known, then there is a fair probability that some part of the text at least is recoverable; articles and letters to the editor may also have survived unnoticed; and the critical reputations of many nineteenth- and twentieth-century authors, when sifted in contemporary journals and newspapers, sometimes differ revealingly from common report.

12. Quotations and references

A quotation always needs a reference, but reference need not always be in the form of a footnote. Footnotes, after all, are on practical grounds a nuisance to author, typist, printer and reader, though at times a necessary nuisance. It is a vulgar error to think them a mark of scholarship. If the discussion concerns a classic text where no large textual disagreements are involved, it is best to use references that apply to most or all editions rather than page-references that merely apply to one's own: Bekker's pagination for Aristotle; act, scene and line for most Elizabethan plays; book and line for *Paradise Lost*; chapter numbers for novels, and so on. Such references, where there is no doubt which work is under discussion, are best tucked in immediately after the quotation rather than as a footnote, e.g. '(ch. 37)'.

As for the texts used in quotation, it may be a vital matter to exercise reasonable caution with them. Ordinary reprints are highly convenient, and for many purposes it is natural to use them. Indeed it might be a practical error to stop the flow of composition in order to verify a detail that could best be left to revision. But many reprints are highly corrupt, and revision should include the verification of quotations and their references against a scholarly edition, where one exists, or against an original text. The warning case of the critic who quoted from the heavily revised New York edition of 1907–9 as an example of Henry

James's early style[1] needs to be kept in mind. Quotation, in any case, should never be indirect: it should derive from its primary source, not from the works of another critic, and the reference too should always be to its primary source.

It is worth adding here that many modern editions and reprints are not merely corrupt but also highly omissive. On a variety of grounds, or as mere oversights, editors and publishers may at times leave out information vital to a literary historian. Modern title-pages often omit subtitles and mottoes without notice, and texts may appear without the author's preface and with internal omissions unmarked. To turn from a convenient modern reprint to an early edition is no mere act of piety, in such circumstances as these, but an act of prudence as well.

If a footnote is unavoidable, it is important to put it in proper form, and above all in a form which is consistent with other footnotes in the same thesis. A work that cites authors and titles in varying order, uses punctuation unsystematically, or cites sometimes the publisher of a book, sometimes its place of publication, sometimes neither and sometimes both, fails to impress the examiner even before he has subjected it to the severer tests of verifying its quotations and references in a library. Any appropriate example of an academic book can be used as an instant reminder of how a reference should be set out, and *The MLA Style Sheet* (New York, 1951) (*see* p. 167, below), which is kept under revision by the Modern Language Association of America, summarizes requirements for the preparation of learned articles and books for the press which, with minor variations, are accepted by more than a hundred journals and by thirty-four university presses. The preferred order is author, title, editor and

[1] Fredson T. Bowers, *Textual and Literary Criticism* (Cambridge, 1959), pp. 166–7, quoting a finding in an anonymous review 'Henry James reprints', *The Times Literary Supplement*, 5 Feb. 1949, p. 96. See also Bruce Harkness, 'Bibliography and the novelistic fallacy', *Studies in Bibliography* (Virginia), xii (1959), reprinted in *A Mirror for Modern Scholars*, edited by Lester A. Beaurline (New York, 1966).

number of volumes, followed by place and date of publication within brackets, and page number, e.g.

> E. D. Leyburn, 'Bishop Berkeley: Metaphysician as Moralist', in *The Age of Johnson: Essays Presented to Chauncey Brewster Tinker*, ed. F. W. Hillies (New Haven, 1949), p. 327.

> Graham Hough, 'The Natural Theology of *In Memoriam*', *Review of English Studies*, xxiii (1947), pp. 244–56.

Since most readers prefer a reference to appear on the same page, footnotes are on the whole to be preferred to endnotes. If the thesis concludes with an alphabetical bibliography in which full details are given, the length of footnotes may be reduced by brief identifying references.

Footnotes exist to support a statement with details which, like those instanced above, are too cumbersome to be inserted in the text itself. They should not be used to contradict or qualify a text, and their use as afterthoughts is to be discouraged. It is better in such cases to rewrite the whole passage; if the qualification is not worth working into the argument itself, then it may well be worth omitting altogether.

A cross-reference exists to save considerable repetition. If the repetition is not considerable, then it is easier for author and reader alike if the details are simply repeated. Terms like *op. cit.*, *ed. cit.* and *ibid.* should be used sparingly, if at all, and only when the work referred to is close at hand and within the same chapter. *Ibid.* should only be used to refer to an item immediately preceding. In general it is far clearer simply to repeat the details in brief; and for this purpose titles may well be 'short', provided they remain recognizable and self-sufficient.

Abbreviation, even when highly systematic and consistent, is perhaps an overrated aid in scholarship. But a thesis which deals exhaustively with a single mass of materials, perhaps by a single author, might gain by a preliminary list which enabled terms like *Works*, *Letters* and *Notebooks* to refer to standard editions. Sigla, or abbreviations (usually initials) of works often referred to, should also be used sparingly, since they only justify themselves where reference is frequent. A thesis on Milton, for instance, might reduce the number and bulk of its footnotes by using *PL* (*Paradise Lost*), *PR* (*Paradise Regained*) and *SA* (*Samson Agonistes*). In such cases abbreviations should be listed alphabetically immediately after the preface.

Appendixes, too, need to be used with caution. They may suit the purposes of certain scholarly books, where a body of information is too vital to be omitted and yet too complex to be inserted in the argument. Sometimes they may suit the purposes of a thesis in a similar way. But they should not be used loosely as an easy excuse for not integrating facts into argument. If the material cannot be used in order, it may be worth asking whether it should be used at all. If it is too interesting to be thrown away, there may be an excellent case for offering it to a learned journal as an article. But the argumentative line of a thesis needs above all else to be clear and visible to the reader, and it should not be cluttered or held in suspense by references to materials which, again and again, are relegated to a conclusion. For similar reasons, the long parenthesis which is itself an entire sentence should be avoided. The alternatives are to omit it altogether or to make a new sentence of it.

Quotations should rarely be long, especially if the work in question is familiar and available. The briefest can best be left in the text of the thesis within inverted commas; longer prose quotations, and all verse quotations more than a line long, should be isolated from the text and indented without inverted commas.

Oblique quotation is best avoided in any work of scholarship. It is usually pointless to summarize a plot, for instance, or any considerable part of a plot, unless of an extremely rare and unfamiliar work; it may even appear insulting to the intelligence of the reader. A literary discussion can hardly be too particular, and direct quotation is an essential tool in the quest for particularity. But it needs to be held in a tight argumentative frame. One refers to an event in a novel, epic or play in order to contribute to the argument, and never for the sake of mere completeness.

45

13. Style

It is reassuring to remind oneself that a thesis is hardly expected to entertain. Sheer dullness, indeed, however much to be regretted, is not a total disqualification. But it should be a matter of concern both to student and to examiner that the work is presented in such a way as to hold the scholarly attention, if not sentence by sentence, then at least page by page. Probably no one cultivates dullness for its own sake, and most scholars would admit to a reasonable duty to avoid it. The demands are fortunately moderate. Eloquence is seldom in prospect here, and is hardly a reasonable ambition: but one can still be crisp and clear. Perhaps the cool, analytical tone of the best traditions of the civil service is a proper mark to aim at: it is a tone that allows, after all, for colour, nuance and wit.

A thesis on a literary subject is exceptionally vulnerable to the charge of illiteracy. It is the sole responsibility of the candidate, if his typist is inaccurate, to correct mistakes of spelling and punctuation before submitting. Elementary mistakes in the use of language are in any case his sole responsibility. No one, not even the supervisor or adviser, can show the student how to write phrase by phrase or sentence by sentence: his own competence in the language is properly a concern of the examiners. What is in question here is not so much a limited matter of rule-observance as a wider and far more significant issue of confidence. In literary history and criticism, the reader will naturally ask whether the critic's own use of language entitles him to be heard with respect when he speaks of the language of others.

Diffuseness is among the commonest faults of academic prose. Graduates who complain of the constriction of the word-limit do not always realize how expendable much of their own language is. A good question to ask of a draft, preferably at the first revision, is whether any given word, phrase or sentence is doing enough work to justify its presence on the page. If it is not, it should be cut. Circumlocutions like 'By this it is not meant to be suggested that . . .' or 'Before considering this question, it is first necessary to consider . . .' should be deleted at a glance. Whole paragraphs which labour a point already established may often be abolished to advantage. Excess of style not only inflates the scale of a thesis beyond the limits of ordinary patience: it also casts reasonable doubts on the intellectual abilities of an author to select and order what is in his mind.

The repetitious use of academic jargon should be shunned. Fashions come and go; but some of the grey apparel of academic prose sadly survives from year to year: 'thus' (especially at the beginning of a sentence); 'meaningful'; 'validity'; 'ambivalence'; 'dichotomy'; 'alienation'; 'relevant' (in the floating or undifferentiated sense); 'structured' and 'patterned'; tired oppositions like 'illusion and reality'; tired colloquialisms like 'to spell out'; and heavy signposting like 'as we have seen' and 'as we shall see'. 'We', indeed, is a term best kept to a minimum in critical prose; and phrases like 'I think' or 'in my opinion' should signify a rare and exceptional emphasis. It is a stylistic crudity to concentrate the main sense of one's prose, again and again, into abstract nouns. It may help in enlivening prose, too, to avoid the excessive use of the passive voice: *for* 'a contrast between the English and the French novel was expressed . . .', *read* 'he contrasted the English and French novel . . .'.

It may be instructive here to attempt to translate a passage of fashionably academic prose into sober and sufficient English, and to consider what, if anything, is lost in the process apart from a sense of mystification. The following is from a recent work of literary criticism:

Then Tragedy is the imitation of an action, and the difference now establishes itself in the very broadest outline between imitating human beings and imitating an action in which humanity is effectively present. Aristotle's composing dramatist, acting out the events of his play, works himself into the pattern of the single distinct *praxis* visible to his mind's eye, struggles to get it physically or emotionally right: this is the process of translating action into plot, *praxis* into *muthos*. In the work of art, of course, his blueprint gestures and movements will be apportioned among a group of stage-figures; differentiation obviously matters, is unavoidable, and therefore falls among the subjects dealt with in Aristotle's text-book.[1]

This might be interpreted:

Tragedy, then, is the imitation of an action. But there is a difference between imitating human beings and imitating an action in which they take part. Aristotle supposes the dramatist, as he writes, to sketch out the events of his play, shaping its *praxis* or action and struggling to get it right in both physical and emotional terms. This is the translation of action into plot, of *praxis* into *muthos*. In the play itself, the dramatist's conception will be divided among a group of actors. The characters they play are bound to be distinguished, and so the *Poetics* deals with character too.

[1] John Jones, *On Aristotle and Greek Tragedy* (London, 1962), p. 36.

14. The bibliography

A final bibliography is usually required, and it will save time to
start a detailed section at once. The list should be an aid to the
student as he works as well as to the examiners as they read;
it will help him to refer without difficulty back to his materials
as he writes. It is far better not to leave it to be a hurried and last-
minute fabrication.

There is no need to seek a false completeness in listing books and
articles which relate to the subject. If a work has for any reason
failed to contribute, then it is proper to omit it. Inclusion in a
list is not in itself evidence that the work has been read, and it
may expose a candidate in the viva to the charge of claiming to
know more than he does. No bibliography, after all, is in the
strictest sense complete, though omissions may need to be justified
on sufficient grounds.

The order of the list is best decided upon at an early stage,
since a belated rearrangement may waste valuable time. An
alphabetical list by author will make reference to the text of the
thesis easier. But if something more ambitious is in view, such
as a comprehensive bibliography of a minor author who is
himself the subject of the thesis, a chronological list might be more
appropriate, at least for the canon of his works.

Entries should appear in a single and consistent form, like footnotes. A headnote such as '*The place of publication, unless it is
London, is cited after the short title*' may save a great many 'Londons'

and make the useful point that titles are not necessarily complete. Unless the thesis is itself on some bibliographical subject, it is not usually necessary to cite the names of publishers at all.

If a work has been revised or enlarged, it is usually best to cite both its first appearance and its final or most recent form, e.g. 'John Carter, *ABC for Book-Collectors* (London, 1952, revised 1967)', and to quote, unless for some special reason, from the revised edition.

15. Presentation

The regulations of many universities prescribe conditions for the presentation of a thesis, and these should be consulted. The examiners will normally require two typed and bound copies; so that it is prudent, in handing the corrected drafts to a typist, to ask for three copies to be made and to preserve one for personal use. There is a grave risk of loss in leaving a draft for long in a unique copy, or in sending it through the post.

Fair copies should be typed double-spaced, apart from indented quotations and footnotes, and with a generous left-hand margin to allow for binding.

Titles are best distinguished by underlining book titles and placing titles of parts of books within single inverted commas, e.g. Pope's Dunciad; Cowper's 'Castaway'. Certain titles which are merely conventional or descriptive are best left undistinguished unless by capitals, e.g. the Sonnets of Shakespeare, the Bible, Gray's Elegy, Johnson's Life of Pope.

Pagination should run continuously from beginning to end. But there may be some risk in confronting a typist with a large manuscript to be typed by a certain date, and it is often more sensible to have fair copies made as the composition of the thesis proceeds; in which case, unless the composition happens to be strictly in final order, it may be necessary to add the final pagination by hand.

16. Works of reference

Most graduates know before they begin that the literature they are studying possesses certain crucial works of reference, and that the main reading room of their university library will help them to extend a working knowledge of these aids, moving outwards from the known towards the unfamiliar. Where nothing is known, Theodore Besterman, *A World Bibliography of Bibliographies*, 4 vols (Geneva, 1939–40, revised 1965–66), which is ordered according to subject, can lead one to the required bibliography—in principle on any subject whatever. For students of French, D. C. Cabeen, *A Critical Bibliography of French Literature* (Syracuse, New York, 1947–), is so far available only as far as 1800. In English, the two principal works of reference are the *Oxford English Dictionary*, 13 vols (Oxford, 1933), of which the supplement is under revision; and the *Cambridge Bibliography of English Literature*, 5 vols (Cambridge, 1940–57), now undergoing total revision as *New CBEL* (Cambridge, 1969–). But *CBEL* excludes the literature of the United States, for which Jacob Blanck, *Bibliography of American Literature* (New Haven, 1955–), an alphabetical list by author, still in progress and primary only, should be consulted. For recent secondary material, it is best to use the annual bibliographies which now appear in various American journals on all periods since the Middle Ages; these are listed at the beginning of each period-section in George Watson, *Concise CBEL 600–1950* (Cambridge, 1958, revised 1965), a one-volume compression of *CBEL*. Biographical dictionaries are also a major aid to the literary student, including *The Dictionary of National Biography*, 21 vols (London, later Oxford, 1885–1909), with supplements to 1950, which is weakest on the Middle Ages and twentieth century; the *Bulletin of the Institute of Historical Research*, however, publishes additions and corrections to *DNB*. *Who Was Who*, which appears decade by decade, is a valuable addition for recent figures; obituaries such as those in the *Gentleman's Magazine* or *The Times*, both stretching back to the eighteenth century, are usually easy to discover if the date of death is known; and they may contain neglected information. So do alumni lists of schools and universities, where they exist.

The *Short-Title Catalogue* of 1926, by A. W. Pollard and G. R. Redgrave, widely known as *STC*, lists the locations of copies of all books published in the British Isles from Caxton to 1640, and *Wing* supplements it for 1641–1700; both are inevitably imperfect, but many libraries have their own lists of STC holdings: all Cambridge college holdings, for instance, are marked in an interleaved copy of *STC* kept in the Anderson Room of the University Library. Other special sources are still incomplete and unpublished: the Cathedral Libraries Catalogue, for instance, listing the locations of books published before 1700 in most of the cathedrals of England and Wales, is still in progress and available only in the British Museum.

Most great libraries, too, possess the vast published catalogues, all with supplements, of the British Museum, the Library of Congress in Washington and the Bibliothèque Nationale, so that it is not necessary to go to London to discover if the British Museum has a book; or to California, or anywhere, to discover an English book published before 1700. Librarians are generous with advice and help. But it is embarrassing to them, and humiliating to oneself, to ask questions which could readily be answered by referring to one of these obvious and available sources.

17. Manuscripts

The original manuscript of an author, or autograph, has a natural fascination in itself; and if it happens to be unpublished, or published in an incomplete or inaccurate way, it may itself form the basis of a thesis, or at least of its most vital part. But to discover new material of considerable literary interest, like the decisive Malory manuscript found at Winchester in 1934, is among the rarest of human experiences, and one can hardly live out a scholarly life in mere expectation. One can, however, live in such a way as to make discovery possible. Alphonse Dain, *Les manuscrits* (Paris, 1949, revised 1964), is an attractive account of the lure of manuscripts for the collector and scholar, mainly classical and medieval in its reference. Latin is dealt with in Paul O. Kristeller, *Latin Manuscript Books before 1600: a List of the Printed Catalogues and Unpublished Inventories of Extant Collectors* (New York, 1960), arranged alphabetically by libraries but without an index of names. The great modern literatures do not yet possess manuscript catalogues of a comprehensive sort, though many published and unpublished catalogues of individual collections exist. Lists of French manuscripts may best be consulted in the Cabinet des Manuscrits in the Bibliothèque Nationale, Paris. English is abundantly if haphazardly provided for in published catalogues: M. R. James, for example, catalogued the manuscripts of Westminster Abbey and the John Rylands Library in Manchester, as well as Eton, Lambeth, Aberdeen University

Library and the Cambridge colleges; J. P. Gilson, *A Student's Guide to the Manuscripts of the British Museum* (London, 1920), and Edmund Craster, *The Western Manuscripts of the Bodleian Library* (Oxford, 1921) are also to be consulted, the last being supplemented in remarkable detail by Margaret Crum, *First-Line Index of English Poetry 1500–1800 in Manuscripts of the Bodleian Library, Oxford*, 2 vols (Oxford, 1969). At the Cambridge University Library the old *Catalogue of Manuscripts*, published in 1856–67 and still worth consulting, is briefly and provisionally supplemented in a pamphlet by A. E. B. Owen, *Summary Guide to Accessions of Western Manuscripts (other than medieval) since 1867* (Cambridge, 1966), and together these serve as an introduction to the Library's unpublished manuscript catalogues and to the manuscripts themselves.

In general the Middle Ages are the best organized. Old English is fully provided for by Neil R. Ker, *Catalogue of Manuscripts Containing Anglo-Saxon* (Oxford, 1957); and British medieval holdings, especially in the smaller collections, are in the course of being described by Ker, *Medieval Manuscripts of British Libraries* (Oxford, 1969–). The last four hundred years, by contrast, call for greater personal initiative. Manuscript holdings in American libraries are summarized state by state in Philip M. Hamer, *A Guide to Archives and Manuscripts in the United States* (New Haven, 1961), which has an index of names. In addition, many libraries and collections, such as the rapidly growing Humanities Research Center at the University of Texas at Austin, have in their keeping unpublished catalogues to which precise inquiries may be directed by letter. All such catalogues and indexes, published or unpublished, may lead one directly to unknown or neglected materials.

Attempts are now being made to organize knowledge of manuscript locations more fully. A Register of Biographical Manuscripts, for instance, was begun in 1959 by the Library Association, London, with the object of recording on slips the manuscript holdings relating to British persons in libraries, record offices and institutions other than the Public Record Office and the six copyright libraries (British Museum, the Bodleian, University Library Cambridge, the National Libraries of Scotland and Wales and Trinity College, Dublin); this project is now being conducted by the City Librarian of Norwich, Mr Philip Hepworth. An entry in the 'Information please' column of *The Times Literary Supplement* or the *Sunday Times*, which are systematically answered by Mr Hepworth, may bring a useful response. The Institute of Historical Research (Senate House, University of London) is recording the migrations of manuscripts and the principal accessions in the Department of Manuscripts in the British Museum, and publishes information in its *Bulletin*.

Archives, too, or the accumulated records of an institution, are now increasingly well organized, and descriptions are now sometimes available in print, such as H. E. Peek and C. P. Hall, *The Archives of the University of Cambridge: an historical introduction* (Cambridge, 1962). In 1945 a National Register of Archives was set up by the Historical Manuscripts Commission, and now contains over 13,000 lists of non-official records in private hands and in record offices and libraries; these lists complement the printed Reports and Calendars published by the Commission since its foundation in 1869. The Register may be consulted at the offices of the Commission (Quality House, Quality Court, Chancery Lane, London W.C.2) or by letter to the Assistant Secretary of the Historical Manuscripts Commission. About 1,000 new lists are added every year, though the bias is still political and economic rather than literary, and the Register is more likely to include entries concerning an author's personal and working papers than manuscripts or proof copies of his works.

For the facilities offered by the Public Record Office, also in Chancery Lane, it is best in the first instance to consult V. H. Galbraith, *An Introduction to the Use of the Public Records* (Oxford, 1934, revised 1952). County record offices, which are now said to exist in every English county but two, may contain unpublished biographical details, especially if the author was born in that county or resident in it; inquiries should first be addressed by letter to the County Archivist at the county or shire hall. The best guide to parish records is W. E. Tate, *The Parish Chest: a study of the records of parochial administration in England* (Cambridge, 1946, revised 1969), with a glossary of terms. For English wills, which may contain information of the career, property and acquaintanceship of an author, there is a brief introduction in B. G. Bouwens, *Wills and their Whereabouts* (London, 1939, revised A. J. Camp, 1963); all wills proved since 1858 are filed at Somerset House, as originals or copies, and may be read on payment of a shilling each.

Discoveries in records and manuscripts are most likely to occur through the patience of a scholar who is prepared to follow his nose, travel to out-of-the-way libraries and recommend himself through his talents and courtesy as a recipient of confidences. Letters to librarians should be precise and specific, since librarians do not usually agree to send long lists of manuscript holdings to unknown correspondents or to photograph materials for them— not even if the inquirer undertakes to pay the expenses for such services. A visit, however, following an exchange of letters with a librarian or archivist and by appointment, will often prove productive.

Courtesy needs to be observed in research which involves manuscripts, whether in requesting permission, in using them or in acknowledging help after a privilege has been enjoyed. Ownership, whether by an institution or private person, confers rights over a manuscript, though not unlimited rights. Most public and university libraries make their manuscript collections available to qualified readers provided certain conditions to ensure the safety of their collections are observed, though they may also require the reader to agree in advance to certain limitations on his use of papers, especially in the matter of publication. This is frequently the case where manuscripts are held in trust or within the terms of a bequest of which the terms are still operative. It is not advisable to protest against such conditions. To allow a reader to see a manuscript is to grant a favour, and it is hardly for the recipient to demand that the favour should be greater than it is. On the other hand, owners occasionally exaggerate the rights they possess, and possession in itself does not automatically confer rights over a text which is already available elsewhere.

Readers of manuscripts should observe a proper respect for the papers they are allowed to see. Ink should not be used at the table where they are read; and if they are loose, it may be important to preserve their existing order. Where manuscripts are used in a thesis, the debt should be acknowledged in the preface, along with other debts of gratitude, and the manuscripts themselves should be recorded in a separate list in the thesis and not in the usual bibliography of books and articles. The list should be as detailed as is practical, and should include the library pressmark, if any. If the list helps towards codifying a body of manuscripts in a collection, and for the first time, then it is an act of courtesy to present a copy of it to the keeper or owner.

Handwriting, which may often prove a prime means of detection, is a study of its own. If the student is in pursuit of manuscripts by his author, it will be natural for him to memorize certain of his idiosyncratic usages. Giles E. Dawson and Laetitia Kennedy-Skipton, *Elizabethan Handwriting 1500–1650* (New York, 1966) is a good introduction to the study of Renaissance hands, especially in England, and includes photographic illustrations; and L. C. Hecter, *The Handwriting of English Documents* (London, 1958, revised 1966) is an excellent general guide, together with Hilda E. P. Grieve, *Examples of English Handwriting 1150–1750* (Chelmsford, 1954) (Essex Record Office Publications).

Students sometimes need to be assured that unpublished materials of literary interest can still exist, and that their use may confer a substantial originality upon their work. Equally, they sometimes need to be urged not to overrate what they have found. Nothing is of significance merely because it is unpublished. The critical spirit needs to work as searchingly and as unceasingly in this matter as in any other.

18. Other theses

It is easy at a distance to exaggerate the help that an existing thesis can give; though to read a thesis recently accepted by one's own university and deposited in the university library may, in cases of nagging doubt, help to explain what standards are required. But unless a thesis is very recent, its value is likely to have been absorbed into some published work, whether a book or an article; and recent theses, unless in the same university, are difficult to learn of in time. Published lists of theses, for these reasons, such as R. D. Altick and W. R. Matthews, *Guide to Doctoral Dissertations in Victorian Literature 1886–1958* (Urbana, 1958), often convey information too old to be useful, unless the subject is a highly specific one like an edition.

In attempting to obtain copies of theses from other universities no general rules apply, and it is best to make inquiries in one's own university library. Inter-library loan and photocopying are usually subject to the written consent of the author, if the work is recent. The policy of British libraries is summarized at the beginning of volumes of *Index to Theses Accepted for Higher Degrees* (Aslib); and of American libraries in *American Doctoral Dissertations* (Association of Research Libraries). Continental universities vary widely in their procedures; some even require publication in a limited edition as part of the requirement for a degree, and at the expense of the doctoral candidate himself. German dissertations on English subjects are listed in Richard Mummendey, *Language and Literature of the Anglo-Saxon Nations as Presented in German Doctoral Dissertations 1885–1950* (Charlottesville, 1954). The most compendious list is now Lawrence F. McNamee, *Dissertations in English and American Literature: theses accepted in American, British and German universities 1865–1964* (New York, 1968), with its first supplement on 1964–68 (New York, 1969).

19. The reproduction of texts

Some libraries will provide microfilms of printed materials in their possession on written request, and even of manuscripts where certain conditions are fulfilled. But microfilm, though compact and easy to send through the post, requires special equipment to read and it is often tiring to the eyes. For many purposes it has now been replaced by xerography (xerox) which makes rapid full-size copies of print or manuscript at low cost. Such copies can be marked and amended for typist or printer, so that the process seems certain to revolutionize the lives of editors by reducing the labours of copying and by guaranteeing faithful copies; though it may be unsuitable for some manuscripts where a high degree of definition is needed, and for these enlargements from microfilm may still be preferable. Xerography, in any case, is sometimes held by librarians to be unsuited to certain kinds of manuscripts which cannot be flattened without risk of damage. Machines are now widely available for use by readers in university and departmental libraries; in Cambridge, for instance, they are available not only in the University Library and in the Modern Languages Faculty, Sidgwick Avenue, but more cheaply in the Scientific Periodicals Library, Bene't Street.

New techniques have also revolutionized the trade in facsimiles, and it may soon make all major literary texts available in photographic copies at low cost. University Microfilms Ltd (St John's Road, Tylers Green, High Wycombe, Buckinghamshire, England;

300 North Zeeb Road, Ann Arbor, Michigan 48106, USA)
already supply xerographic copies of all *STC* and of many *Wing*
books—of most books published in the British Isles from Caxton
to 1700, in fact—as well as many published since; and many
other reprint series are now flourishing. For the literary historian,
and more especially for the aspiring editor, the significance of these
technical advances is hardly yet to be measured.

20. Supervision

Universities assign a graduate student to a supervisor, usually a senior member of the department or faculty to which the student belongs, who undertakes responsibility for his course of study. In American universities the terms 'adviser' and 'sponsor' are more usual. The relation of a graduate to his supervisor is rightly various in the highest degree, and no attempt will be made here to describe an ideal. Certain misconceptions, however, may be laid to rest.

A graduate is admitted to research because a university believes him to be already capable of performing it, or of finding out how to do so. It is no part of a supervisor's duty to explain how research is done. Where explanations exist in print, it is natural that the attention of students should be drawn to them; and many universities offer graduate classes on research methods. But the tasks of the supervisor are not so much to inform as to give general advice and moral encouragement, and to warn against rash assumptions in argument; and he should warn early, since such assumptions, if carried over from chapter to chapter, could on occasion vitiate an entire thesis. Above all, he may impose a sense of order in the use of time, of a sort that all authors except the most self-disciplined seem to require. Perhaps the most useful function of the supervisor lies here, in establishing agreements with his pupil on the date of delivery of the first draft of a given chapter. Such agreements, which are necessarily two-sided, can give the graduate points of fixity in an existence which might otherwise become demoralizingly unspecified.

The supervisor advises on first drafts. He may not, however, unless for some special reason, see the finished thesis, so that decisions concerning what use in detail to make of his advice are properly the business of the student, who is free to ignore such advice at his own risk. The student may believe, indeed, and perhaps for good reason, that he knows more about his topic than his supervisor. There need be nothing arrogant in such a view: it is not difficult, after all, to become a world authority on a matter of confined interest, and if the subject is of that sort it may be entirely natural for the student after a few weeks of research to know more about it than anybody on earth. On the other hand, the student is less likely to know more than his supervisor about literary studies in general. It is at the point where the discussion ceases to be narrow and enters into a wider context that he will find the advice of his supervisor most suggestive.

Most supervisors are busy scholars engaged in undergraduate as well as graduate teaching, and in their own research as well. If it is unrealistic to suppose that they will show the student how research is done, it is equally unrealistic to think of them as freely available at all hours. Being literary men, they will often respond more readily to letters than to telephone calls, and may dislike situations of urgency which could with foresight have been avoided. But they often form the closest link which the graduate student has with senior members of his university, and their advice may well be asked in making contact with their colleagues. Nor is it usually offensive to suggest a change of direction. Many supervisors recognize, often before their pupils, that a new tendency in the thesis, or a new element in personal relations, constitutes a case for change, and such changes are in no way extraordinary.

21. Classes and seminars

Graduate classes and seminars are now common in the larger universities, and are usually conducted as an exchange between a group of students and one or two senior instructors. Their subject may be methods of research and bibliography or (if the size and composition of a graduate school encourages it) an historical period, or a theme of common interest to a group of students. Such classes are mostly listed in the programme or lecture-list, and they form one of the easiest ways by which a new graduate, and especially one from another university, can temper the isolation of his position and form friendships with other graduates and with senior members. He is, in any case, altogether free to start his own discussion-groups with others working in similar fields.

It is a mistake to grudge time spent in acquiring techniques which are not immediately useful. Graduates sometimes avoid classes on the principle that they have no time for anything but the thesis; but a healthy intellectual life can hardly be maintained on a single continuum of interest. The mind needs to be turned over, and a state of intellectual mesmerism is bad for the thesis as well as bad for the student. Lectures which have nothing to do with the thesis, and especially lectures on kindred disciplines such as the other arts, philosophy or social history, may invigorate his mind and direct it into unexpected connections. A knowledge of the elements of bibliography, too, is useful in a general sense, independently of whether it helps the thesis or not. The viva or orals, in any case, may ask of the student something more than the matter of the thesis alone: it may call upon him to hold views about the relation between what he has written and the intellectual issues that converge upon it. Graduates who protest that they have no time for such activities should ask themselves whether they are not missing the best things the university has to offer. Time, after all, is not simple and finite, and it can be used in leisure as well as in work. If there is time to read a newspaper or see a film, then there is time to hear a lecture which has nothing to do with the preoccupations of the moment.

A total emphasis on the thesis, too, will leave the graduate professionally embarrassed after he has achieved his qualification. He may find himself embittered by a sense of loss at the thought of what he failed to do in his university, of opportunities to listen and to learn which he will never enjoy again. And if he becomes a university teacher, he may realize with appalling suddenness that the thesis provides him, at the most, with one set of lectures to deliver, and that he is expected to teach the literature of several centuries. It will be too late then to regret the general education which he could once have had for nothing.

22. Learning a language

In many American universities the acquisition of one or more foreign languages may be required of graduate students by means of classwork and examination. In European universities such competence is more often assumed, and it may be among the qualifications required for admission into a programme of research. This will usually depend on the subject in view. If it is a comparative subject, then it is not usually thought practical for a graduate to attempt to acquire the necessary linguistic competence from a condition of total ignorance. If the topic requires an advanced knowledge of German, for instance, of a kind that a professional Germanist possesses, then it is less than realistic to suppose that one can achieve such a level of competence within two or three years.

Most subjects, however, are not comparative, and the linguistic needs of a graduate are often more moderate than this. He may merely seek a knowledge of German, for instance, sufficient to read certain secondary sources such as scholarly articles. There is no need to seek or to claim too much in such matters. Even a smattering of a language may be very much better than nothing. To learn the Greek alphabet, for example, along with some elements of Greek grammar and a modest vocabulary, is a task that may take only a few weeks. It will not enable one to read Greek, but it will make it possible to use a Greek-English dictionary and a Greek-English text such as those in the Loeb Classical Library, and it will help the student of English to read an English etymological dictionary with closer understanding. If a mere smattering of Greek can do as much as that, then it is plainly worth having; and it may later lead to something more. The next step is a reading knowledge; and the next after that, if the language is a living one, is an ability to speak it and to write it. Only the most gifted, however, are likely to take this final step without special instruction or a period of residence.

Graduates do not always notice the resources already to hand when they realize they must acquire a smattering or a reading knowledge of a language. Universities often provide such teaching facilities at small cost or none, so that it may not be necessary to enlist expensive help from an individual teacher. If the graduate has taken a language at school as far as matriculation, for example, he may find that the classes in composition provided by his university for freshmen, or even the more advanced classes, are available to him for nothing on request to the instructor. A further possibility, especially if he is a beginner, may be found in the language laboratories which many universities have recently created. These enable the student to learn a foreign language from scratch, or improve an existing knowledge, by means of a pre-recorded programme of question and answer. Progress depends on the concentration of effort, and it should be emphasized that an excessively concentrated learning programme may lead to a process of rapid forgetting as easily as to rapid acquisition. A moderate programme, however, of up to ten hours a week should normally lead to a competent reading knowledge in less than six months. In that case the student will usually find that he can read a literary text with moderate efficiency and with the help of a dictionary, though an ability to speak and to write will require a longer process than this. Only living languages are available by laboratory methods.

Many graduates, being highly literate, prefer to learn a language in the more traditional manner from books and in their own time. There is now an abundance of books of phased learning by which a solitary beginner can acquire knowledge of a grammatical system and a reasonable vocabulary over a period of months, or by which he can brush up an existing but elementary competence. The next stage may take him to a bilingual text, especially if such texts exist in his own field of literary study; in ancient Greek and Latin this provision is very wide, as it is in certain areas of medieval literature; in modern languages it is rapidly increasing. One useful technique is to read a section or chapter rapidly through in translation in order to grasp the general substance, and then return to read slowly the original text of the same passage. This technique will reduce, though not remove, the need to refer to a dictionary, and encourage the learner with a sense of progress. If poems, or even prose passages, can be learned by heart, this will allow him to live with literary masterpieces in his mind and to sense their fullness to a degree which rapid reading alone could not give.

23. The viva or orals

The viva or oral examination has now been abandoned by some universities in the United States, so that the completion of a thesis to the satisfaction of the advisor may now represent the successful end of a doctoral programme. In American universities, however, the thesis is normally only a part of the requirements for a doctorate. Regulations vary widely, and applicants may assure themselves of the details by consulting published handbooks, where they exist, or by writing to departmental chairmen.

In European universities, the viva is normally required after the first submission, though it may be waived where a thesis is submitted for the second time or even, if the examiners agree, for the first, where compelling reasons such as difficulties of travel apply. These are commonly matters within the discretion of the examiners, who retain the right to insist upon a viva; and candidates do not have the right to demand such a concession or to ask of the Faculty or Department to obtain it for them. The normal expectation is that a viva should occur; and it is worth noting what this expectation involves.

First, it is in the interest of the candidate to notify his Faculty or Department as soon as he can of the date by which he will submit copies of his thesis. The appointment of examiners may prove to be a difficult matter, especially if the thesis is long; and the longer the notice given, the shorter the delay between submission and viva.

Second, the candidate should anticipate a period of months between the appointment of examiners and the viva itself. If he remains in the country, this delay may be a matter of little concern to him. But if his plans require him to go abroad, then the responsibility for any delays´ or inconvenience this may cause are entirely his own. Universities cannot guarantee the prompt attention of examiners to a thesis, or commit examiners to waiving a viva; and they do not pay the fares and expenses of doctoral candidates.

In British universities the viva is normally a private interview between the candidate and two examiners. One is often internal and one external; the identity of the examiners is not known to the candidate until after the thesis has been submitted. In some continental universities, by contrast, the *soutenance de thèse* may be open to the public or, at least, to other members of the university. There are also wide divergences of custom in the declaration of the result. In some universities the examiners are permitted to inform the candidate of the verdict during the viva: in others, the examiners are required to inform the university authorities first, who then inform the candidate. Success and failure are not the only possible verdicts: if the thesis is of intermediate value, the candidate may be offered an intermediate degree, such as mastership instead of a doctorate, or perhaps the opportunity to revise and resubmit. Such resubmission is normally allowed only once.

It is natural to expect examiners in the viva to pay attention both to narrow questions of formal accuracy, especially in quotations and references, and to the wider issues raised by the thesis; and these issues may be wider than the thesis itself, since it is within the rights and duties of the examiners to ascertain whether the candidate understands the implications of what he has written and possesses a general competence in the historical period in which his work is set. They may be impressed at the viva by evidence of an active and continuing commitment on the part of the candidate to the topic in particular and to literary studies in general; such evidence can sometimes act favourably, and even decisively, where the thesis is open to question on other grounds. It is naïve to assume that the occasion is primarily commendatory: on the contrary, it is exploratory and critical, and a candidate may expect questions subversive of the assumptions of his thesis and neglectful of what may seem to him its best elements. It is equally naïve to think of the viva as a trial in a personal sense. In the end it is the thesis that is being judged rather than the candidate, and examiners are bound to grant a degree if the thesis is of sufficient standard, and to refuse it if it is not, regardless of whether the candidate acquits himself well or badly in interview. It is only in borderline instances, for the most part, in which a viva is decisive: it may then provide an opportunity for the candidate to justify what appear to be defects in his thesis and to defend it, perhaps, against imputations of plagiarism or inaccuracy.

The viva, where it is decisive, tests an ability to respond rather than a willingness to agree over the wide range of questions on which intelligent men may differ. A ready, talkative response is likely to impress: an apathetic, dismissive or truculent one less so. That the candidate holds opinions similar to those of the examiners is of little significance in itself. What matters is that he should show a readiness to consider objections with an open mind and to argue his case, or a modified version of it, with courage and vivacity. Disagreement is the stuff of scholarship, after all; and it is entirely natural, even with the most successful thesis, that a viva should end on a friendly agreement to differ.

24. Publication

It is right to expect a thesis to be published in some form, in whole or in part, and helpful to consider the prospect well in advance. A thesis prepared with a view to eventual publication is likely to prove more publishable for just that reason; and if composed with an eye to readership and fortified by the literary discipline that a sense of readership can give, it is likely to prove a better thesis as well.

It is also true, however, that a thesis is seldom publishable as it stands. In essence it is an exhibition piece, designed to prove to the scholars who examine it that the candidate is both competent and original. Several species of change often need to be made before it can reasonably be offered to a publisher:

(a) a reduction of the factual evidence offered, especially in foot-notes;

(b) a reduction of references in the argument to secondary materials, i.e. to the works of other critics and scholars;

(c) a reduction of supporting arguments which exist to bolster an existing case;

(d) a clearer and bolder statement of objectives, especially in the first and last paragraphs of chapters.

These requirements, among others, arise from a marked difference in readership. The reader of a book is trustful in a way an examiner has no business to be. If he did not believe that the author knew his subject, he would probably not have bought or borrowed the book at all. He is less concerned—perhaps totally unconcerned—about the state of the subject, and indifferent to disagreements among scholars unless they are presented in an exceptionally arresting way. And he often wants to be told, and in the plainest terms, what the subject is for and how it helps to understand some wider issue, such as the total period in which it is set. In a book the props and flying buttresses that often support a thesis need to be stripped away, and the intellectual form left visible to the reader as a clean, bare and memorable fabric of argument.

If the thesis seems to promise a book, the author cannot reasonably avoid considering the state of the market. He may decide to put the matter in the hands of a literary agent who understands the literary market well. Failing that, he should visit a bookshop and consider which publisher is likely to be most hospitable to the work he has in hand. *The Writers' and Artists' Year Book*, which appears annually, will supply further information, including addresses of publishers and information about agents and copyright.

An approach is best made to a publisher or agent by submitting a draft table of contents of the proposed work and an estimate of its length. If the publisher is attracted, he will then ask to see the book when it is finished, and may also ask in advance for some modification in the plan: a clearer order for the chapters, the addition of an introduction that places the work in a wider perspective, or of a final bibliography that will enhance the value of the book for students. Titles, whether of the thesis or book itself, or of its individual chapters, should be severely descriptive, with a view to helping the reader to find his way about. An author may be witty in his text, but hardly on the title-page or in the table of contents, where the allusive and the facetious are always out of place.

If the work can be offered as a member of an existing publisher's series, the chances of acceptance may be greater; and in that case application should be made not to the publisher but to the General Editor of the series.

73

Articles, unlike books, may well be undertaken in the course of writing a thesis, and nothing could be better for the morale of the student or for his professional standing than to have one or more articles accepted before he submits his thesis. Learned journals, which do not usually pay for contributions and which may even charge authors for offprints, are hospitable to scholarly articles provided they are not excessively long, are set out in a clear order without the need for laborious editing, and fit the general character of the journal. It is for the contributor to decide which journal his article will best fit; but if he is already working on articles on his own subject, he may find he knows the answer without effort. Other forms of publication, such as the London weeklies and the BBC, are more difficult for the beginner to achieve but may reward him well. There is no good reason, in any case, to take a condescending view of literary journalism: Humphry House's *All in Due Time* (London, 1955), which collects his broadcasts and weekly reviews, is one of many examples of how sensitive and original such criticism can be.

25. Application to research

The demands of university departments vary widely in the information they require from applicants for research. Full details of the existing qualifications of applicants, and letters of recommendation from previous teachers, are usually required. Applicants should consult the regulations of the university to which they wish to apply, if these are published, or write for details. Some of the larger graduate schools now issue leaflets on request, and the Higher Education Advisory Centre (Enfield College of Technology, Queensway, Enfield, Middlesex) issues a series of publications entitled *Graduate Studies* on the courses provided by British universities (*Volume 1*: *Humanities*); the Centre now answers postal inquiries from a computerized information service.

In the case of most British universities, application is best made as early as March for the academic year that begins in the following October. Many American universities, on the other hand, now require applications not later than the end of December for an academic year beginning in the following September. European graduates wishing to undertake graduate programmes in the United States may, for this reason, find it advisable to apply to begin a year after their graduation. American programmes, unlike the European, will usually involve the graduate in an element of classwork and examination, at least in the form of term-papers. Some universities hold qualifying examinations for graduate students early in their careers in research.

Requirements concerning the definition of subject at the time of application also differ widely from university to university and from department to department. Some departments admit on evidence of personal competence alone, and leave the question of definition to a later stage. Others, including London and Cambridge, often require a defined topic, and even an outline of that topic in the form of an essay, as evidence of competence. American universities do not usually demand an exact statement, though such a statement may nonetheless strengthen an application, especially one made from a distance.

The range of graduate qualifications offered also differs widely, and the doctorate is far from being the only available degree in many universities. Oxford and Cambridge do not grant M.A.s on examination, as a number of other British universities do, but they provide intermediate degrees such as B.Litt. or M.Litt. Some universities do not permit registration for a doctorate in the first instance. Application should first be made to the university or departmental authority, such as the Board of Graduate Studies at Cambridge (Old Press Site, Mill Lane); or, at Oxford, to a college authority; in successful applications to Cambridge a college affiliation will often follow. In the case of the University of London, application should be made to the Registrar of the School of the university to which entrance is sought, and the onus of acceptance rests entirely with the authorities of the School.

Graduate students may be permitted to engage in teaching within the universities in which they are conducting research. Such permission is often conditional on university regulations: at Cambridge, for instance, graduate students are not permitted to teach for more than six hours a week.

A note on further reading

Jacques Barzun and Henry F. Graff, *The Modern Researcher* (New York, 1957) is a long survey of the possibilities and perils of literary and historical research. R. D. Altick, *The Art of Literary Research* (New York, 1963) is a somewhat lighter but still wide-ranging discussion; and his *The Scholar Adventurers* (New York, 1950, corrected 1966) is a collection of accounts of actual examples of literary discovery. James Thorpe, *Literary Scholarship: a handbook for advanced students of English and American literature* (Boston, 1964) is a manual suited to the conditions of American graduate schools. G. Kitson Clark, *Guide for Research Students Working on Historical Subjects* (Cambridge, 1958), is a brief and succinct booklet almost as enlightening to the literary student as to the historian.

On the details of presentation, W. R. Parker, *The MLA Style Sheet* (New York, 1951, etc.), below, and *Notes on the Presentation of Theses on Literary Subjects* (London, 1952, etc.), which is published with the sanction of the Board of the Oxford English Faculty, are both helpful summaries of pamphlet length. The German equivalent to these is Georg Bangen, *Die schriftliche Form germanistischer Arbeiten* (Stuttgart, 1962).

For the mysteries of bibliography, both enumerative and analytical, the best introduction is John Carter, *ABC for Book-Collectors* (London, 1952, revised 1967), a witty guide set out in alphabetical order. R. B. McKerrow, *An Introduction to Bibliography for Literary Students* (Oxford, 1927, corrected 1928) is a more advanced and technical study with useful appendices on abbreviations and contractions in early printed books, Latinized versions of place-names and Elizabethan handwriting. On textual criticism, Paul Maas, *Textual Criticism* (Oxford, 1958) is a succinct account of the problems of manuscript transmission in classical scholarship; a briefer statement will be found in his article 'Textual criticism' in the *Oxford Classical Dictionary* (Oxford, 1949, revised 1970). English bibliographical scholarship has been mainly concentrated on the textual problem in Shakespeare, at least before Fredson T. Bowers, *Principles of Bibliographical Description* (Princeton, 1949), where the emphasis shifts towards the nineteenth and twentieth centuries. On preparing articles for learned journals, R. B. McKerrow, 'Form and matter in the publication of research', *Review of English Studies* (1940), reprinted below, is a rare disclosure by an editor of his preferences in choosing articles for publication. George Watson, *The Study of Literature* (London, 1969) interprets the new role of literary history, including the art of editing and the prospects of collaboration with linguistics, sociology, psychoanalysis, the history of ideas and cultural history; R. S. Crane, *The Idea of the Humanities and Other Essays*, 2 vols (Chicago, 1967), includes valuable discussions of the conduct of criticism, notably the 1957 lecture 'Criticism as enquiry: or the perils of the "high priori road" '.

For further reading, the chapter 'Literary scholarship', largely by H. T. Meserole, in F. W. Bateson, *A Guide to English Literature* (London, 1965, revised 1967), is a brief and pointed account of published aids to research.

Part Two

Aids to research

The following eight essays are collected here as significant aids to literary research. R. G. Collingwood reveals in an autobiographical form the nature of original intellectual discovery, and illustrates it from his own experience as a philosopher and historian. R. W. Chapman, as editor and bibliographer, describes how in his lifetime some of the techniques of textual criticism, already familiar in classical studies, were applied for the first time to modern literatures such as English. M. R. James, Provost of Eton College, offers a history of Western manuscripts in outline and explains how to seek them out. Seymour de Ricci, in the introductory lecture in a series on English collectors, describes the growth of great private collections in England since the sixteenth century. John Carter, in a brief essay on the format of books, describes how folios, quartos and octavos are to be distinguished. W. W. Greg, in a classic paper by a bibliographer, explains on what principles to choose and edit a text. R. B. McKerrow, as editor of the Review of English Studies, describes his experience in conducting a learned journal and advises authors on how to present their articles for publication. And The MLA Style Sheet, in its latest revision, summarizes the acceptable conventions of presentation for publication.

R G Collingwood

1. *Question and answer*[*]

A year or two after the outbreak of war, I was living in London and working with a section of the Admiralty Intelligence Division in the rooms of the Royal Geographical Society. Every day I walked across Kensington Gardens and past the Albert Memorial. The Albert Memorial began by degrees to obsess me. Like Wordsworth's Leech-gatherer, it took on a strange air of significance; it seemed

> Like one whom I had met with in a dream;
> Or like a man from some far region sent,
> To give me human strength, by apt admonishment.

Everything about it was visibly misshapen, corrupt, crawling, verminous; for a time I could not bear to look at it, and passed with averted eyes; recovering from this weakness, I forced myself to look, and to face day by day the question: a thing so obviously, so incontrovertibly, so indefensibly bad, why had Scott done it? To say that Scott was a bad architect was to burke the problem with a tautology; to say that there was no accounting for tastes was to evade it by *suggestio falsi*. What relation was there, I began to ask myself, between what he had done and what he had tried to do? Had he tried to produce a beautiful thing; a thing, I meant, which we should have thought beautiful? If so, he had of course

[*] From *An Autobiography* (Oxford: Clarendon Press, 1939), chapter v, pp. 29-43.

failed. But had he perhaps been trying to produce something different? If so, he might possibly have succeeded. If I found the monument merely loathsome, was that perhaps my fault? Was I looking in it for qualities it did not possess, and either ignoring or despising those it did?

I will not try to describe everything I went through in what, for many months, continued to be my daily communings with the Albert Memorial. Of the various thoughts that came to me in those communings I will only state one: a further development of a thought already familiar to me.

My work in archaeology, as I have said, impressed upon me the importance of the 'questioning activity' in knowledge; and this made it impossible for me to rest contented with the intuitionist theory of knowledge favoured by the 'realists'. The effect of this on my logic was to bring about in my mind a revolt against the current logical theories of the time, a good deal like that revolt against the scholastic logic which was produced in the minds of Bacon and Descartes by reflection on the experience of scientific research, as that was taking new shape in the late sixteenth and early seventeenth centuries. The *Novum Organum* and the *Discours de la Méthode* began to have a new significance for me. They were the classical expressions of a principle in logic which I found it necessary to restate: the principle that a body of knowledge consists not of 'propositions', 'statements', 'judgements', or whatever name logicians use in order to designate assertive acts of thought (or what in those acts is asserted: for 'knowledge' means both the activity of knowing and what is known), but of these together with the questions they are meant to answer; and that a logic in which the answers are attended to and the questions neglected is a false logic.

I will try to indicate, briefly as the nature of this book requires (for it is an autobiography, not a work on logic), the way in which this notion developed in my mind as I reflected day by day upon the Albert Memorial. I know that what I am going to say is very controversial, and that almost any reader who is already something of a logician will violently disagree with it. But I shall make no attempt to forestall his criticisms. So far as he belongs to any logical school now existing, I think I know already what they will be, and it is because I am not convinced by them that I am writing this chapter. I shall not use the word 'judgement', like the so-called 'idealistic' logicians, or Cook Wilson's word 'statement': the thing denoted by these words I shall call a 'proposition': so that this word will always in this chapter denote a logical, not a linguistic, entity.

I began by observing that you cannot find out what a man means by simply studying his spoken or written statements, even though he has spoken or written with perfect command of language and perfectly truthful intention. In order to find out his meaning you must also know what the question was (a question in his own mind, and presumed by him to be in yours) to which the thing he has said or written was meant as an answer.

It must be understood that question and answer, as I conceived them, were strictly correlative. A proposition was not an answer, or at any rate could not be the right answer, to any question which might have been answered otherwise. A highly detailed and particularized proposition must be the answer, not to a vague and generalized question, but to a question as detailed and particularized as itself. For example, if my car will not go, I may spend an hour searching for the cause of its failure. If, during this hour, I take out number one plug, lay it on the engine, turn the starting-handle, and watch for a spark, my observation 'number one plug is all right' is an answer not to the question, 'Why won't my car go?' but to the question, 'Is it because number one plug is not sparking that my car won't go?' Any one of the various experiments I make during the hour will be the finding of an answer to some such detailed and particularized question. The question, 'Why won't my car go?' is only a kind of summary of all these taken together. It is not a separate question asked at a separate time, nor is it a sustained question which I continue to ask for the whole hour together. Consequently, when I say 'Number one plug is all right', this observation does not record one more failure to answer the hour-long question, 'What is wrong with my car?' It records a success in answering the three-minutes-long question, 'Is the stoppage due to failure in number one plug?'

In passing, I will note (what I shall return to later on) that this principle of correlativity between question and answer disposes of a good deal of clap-trap. People will speak of a savage as 'confronted by the eternal problem of obtaining food'. But what really confronts him is the problem, quite transitory like all things human, of spearing this fish, or digging up this root, or finding blackberries in this wood.

My next step was to apply this principle to the idea of contradiction. The current logic maintained that two propositions might, simply as propositions, contradict one another, and that by examining them simply as propositions you could find out whether they did so or not. This I denied. If you cannot tell what a proposition means unless you know what question it is meant to answer, you will mistake its meaning if you make a mistake about that question. One symptom of mistaking the meaning of a proposition is thinking that it contradicts another proposition which in fact it does not contradict. No two propositions, I saw, can contradict one another unless they are answers to the same question. It is therefore impossible to say of a man, 'I do not know what the question is which he is trying to answer, but I can see that he is contradicting himself.'

The same principle applied to the idea of truth. If the meaning of a proposition is relative to the question it answers, its truth must be relative to the same thing, Meaning, agreement and contradiction, truth and falsehood, none of these belonged to propositions in their own right, propositions by themselves; they belonged only to propositions as the answers to questions: each proposition answering a question strictly correlative to itself.

Here I parted company with what I called propositional logic, and its offspring the generally recognized theories of truth. According to propositional logic (under which denomination I include the so-called 'traditional' logic, the 'idealistic' logic of the eighteenth and nineteenth centuries, and the 'symbolic' logic of the nineteenth and twentieth), truth or falsehood, which are what logic is chiefly concerned with, belongs to propositions as such. This doctrine was often expressed by calling the proposition the 'unit of thought', meaning that if you divide it up into parts such as subject, copula, predicate, any of these parts taken singly is not a complete thought, that is, not capable of being true or false.

It seemed to me that this doctrine was a mistake due to the early partnership between logic and grammar. The logician's proposition seemed to me a kind of ghostly double of the grammarian's sentence, just as in primitive speculation about the mind people imagine minds as ghostly doubles of bodies. Grammar recognizes a form of discourse called the sentence, and among sentences, as well as other kinds which serve as the verbal expressions of questions, commands, &c., one kind which express statements. In grammatical phraseology, these are indicative sentences; and logicians have almost always tried to conceive the 'unit of thought', or that which is either true or false, as a kind of logical 'soul' whose linguistic 'body' is the indicative sentence.

This attempt to correlate the logical proposition with the grammatical indicative sentence has never been altogether satisfactory. There have always been people who saw that the true 'unit of thought' was not the proposition but something more complex in which the proposition served as answer to a question. Not only Bacon and Descartes, but Plato and Kant, come to mind as examples. When Plato described thinking as a 'dialogue of the soul with itself', he meant (as we know from his own dialogues) that it was a process of question and answer, and that of these two elements the primacy belongs to the questioning activity, the Socrates within us. When Kant said that it takes a wise man to know what questions he can reasonably ask, he was in effect repudiating a merely propositional logic and demanding a logic of question and answer.

Even apart from this, however, logic has never been able to

assert a *de facto* one-one relation between propositions and indicative sentences. It has always maintained that the words actually used by a man on a given occasion in order to express his thought may be 'elliptical' or 'pleonastic' or in some other way not quite in accordance with the rule that one sentence should express one proposition. It is generally held, again, that indicative sentences in a work of fiction, professing to be that and nothing more, do not express propositions. But when these and other qualifications have been made, this can be described as the central doctrine of propositional logic; that there is, or ought to be, or in a well-constructed and well-used language would be,[1] a one-one correspondence between propositions and indicative sentences, every indicative sentence expressing a proposition, and a proposition being defined as the unit of thought, or that which is true or false.

This is the doctrine which is presupposed by all the various well-known theories of truth. One school of thought holds that a proposition is either true or false simply in itself, trueness or falseness being qualities of propositions. Another school holds that to call it true or false is to assert a relation of 'correspondence' or 'non-correspondence' between it and something not a proposition, some 'state of things' or 'fact'. A third holds that to call it true or false is to assert a relation between it and other propositions with which it 'coheres' or fails to 'cohere'. And, since in those days there were pragmatists, a fourth school should be mentioned, holding (at least according to some of their pronouncements) that to call a proposition true or false is to assert the utility or inutility of believing it.

All these theories of truth I denied. This was not very original of me; any one could see, after reading Joachim's *Nature of Truth*, that they were all open to fatal objections. My reason for denying them, however, was not that they were severally open

[1] Hence that numerous and frightful offspring of propositional logic out of illiteracy, the various attempts at a 'logical language', beginning with the pedantry of the text-books about 'reducing a proposition to logical form', and ending, for the present, in the typographical jargon of *Principia Mathematica*.

to objections, but that they all presupposed what I have called
the principle of propositional logic; and this principle I denied
altogether.

For a logic of propositions I wanted to substitute what I called
a logic of question and answer. It seemed to me that truth, if that
meant the kind of thing which I was accustomed to pursue in my
ordinary work as a philosopher or historian—truth in the sense
in which a philosophical theory or an historical narrative is called
true, which seemed to me the proper sense of the word—was
something that belonged not to any single proposition, nor even,
as the coherence-theorists maintained, to a complex of propositions taken together; but to a complex consisting of questions and
answers. The structure of this complex had, of course, never been
studied by propositional logic; but with help from Bacon,
Descartes, and others I could hazard a few statements about it.
Each question and each answer in a given complex had to be
relevant or appropriate, had to 'belong' both to the whole and
to the place it occupied in the whole. Each question had to 'arise';
there must be that about it whose absence we condemn when we
refuse to answer a question on the ground that it 'doesn't arise'.
Each answer must be 'the right' answer to the question it professes
to answer.

By 'right' I do not mean 'true'. The 'right' answer to a question
is the answer which enables us to get ahead with the process of
questioning and answering. Cases are quite common in which the
'right' answer to a question is 'false'; for example, cases in which a
thinker is following a false scent, either inadvertently or in order
to construct a *reductio ad absurdum*. Thus, when Socrates asks
(Plato, *Republic*, 333 B) whether as your partner in a game of
draughts you would prefer to have a just man or a man who knows
how to play draughts, the answer which Polemarchus gives—
'a man who knows how to play draughts'—is the right answer.
It is 'false', because it presupposes that justice and ability to play
draughts are comparable, each of them being a 'craft', or special-
ized form of skill. But it is 'right', because it constitutes a link,

and a sound one, in the chain of questions and answers by which the falseness of that presupposition is made manifest.

What is ordinarily meant when a proposition is called 'true', I thought, was this: (a) the proposition belongs to a question-and-answer complex which as a whole is 'true' in the proper sense of the word; (b) within this complex it is an answer to a certain question; (c) the question is what we ordinarily call a sensible or intelligent question, not a silly one, or in my terminology it 'arises'; (d) the proposition is the 'right' answer to that question.

If this is what is meant by calling a proposition 'true', it follows not only that you cannot tell whether a proposition is 'true' or 'false' until you know what question it was intended to answer, but also that a proposition which in fact is 'true' can always be thought 'false' by any one who takes the trouble to excogitate a question to which it would have been the wrong answer, and convinces himself that this was the question it was meant to answer. And a proposition which in fact is significant can always be thought meaningless by any one who convinces himself that it was intended as an answer to a question which, if it had really been intended to answer it, it would not have answered at all, either rightly or wrongly. Whether a given proposition is true or false, significant or meaningless, depends on what question it was meant to answer; and any one who wishes to know whether a given proposition is true or false, significant or meaningless, must find out what question it was meant to answer.

Now, the question 'To what question did So-and-so intend this proposition for an answer?' is an historical question, and therefore cannot be settled except by historical methods. When So-and-so wrote in a distant past, it is generally a very difficult one, because writers (at any rate good writers) always write for their contemporaries, and in particular for those who are 'likely to be interested', which means those who are already asking the question to which an answer is being offered; and consequently a writer very seldom explains what the question is that he is trying to answer. Later on, when he has become a 'classic' and his contemporaries are all long dead, the question has been forgotten; especially if the answer he gave was generally acknowledged to be the right answer; for in that case people stopped asking the question, and began asking the question that next arose. So the question asked by the original writer can only be reconstructed historically, often not without the exercise of considerable historical skill.

"Sblood!' says Hamlet, 'do you think I am easier to be played on than a pipe?' Those eminent philosophers, Rosencrantz and Guildenstern, think *tout bonnement* that they can discover what the *Parmenides* is about by merely reading it; but if you took them to the south gate of Housesteads and said, 'Please distinguish the various periods of construction here, and explain what purpose the builders of each period had in mind,' they would protest 'Believe me, I cannot.' Do they think the *Parmenides* is easier to understand than a rotten little Roman fort? 'Sblood!

It follows, too, and this is what especially struck me at the time, that whereas no two propositions can be in themselves mutually contradictory, there are many cases in which one and the same pair of propositions are capable of being thought either that or the opposite, according as the questions they were meant to answer are reconstructed in one way or in another. For example, metaphysicians have been heard to say 'the world is both one and many'; and critics have not been wanting who were stupid enough to accuse them of contradicting themselves, on the abstractly logical ground that 'the world is one' and 'the world is many' are mutually contradictory propositions. A great deal of the popular dislike of metaphysics is based on grounds of this sort, and is ultimately due to critics who, as we say, did not know what the men they criticized were talking about; that is, did not know what questions their talk was intended to answer; but, with the ordinary malevolence of the idle against the industrious, the ignorant against the learned, the fool against the wise man, wished to have it believed that they were talking nonsense.

Suppose, instead of talking about the world, the metaphysician were talking about the contents of a small mahogany box with a sliding top; and suppose he said, 'The contents of this box are both one thing and many things.' A stupid critic may think that he is offering two incompatible answers to a single question, 'Are the contents of this box one x or many x's?' But the critic has reconstructed the question wrong. There were two questions: (*a*) Are the contents of this box one set of chessmen or many sets? (*b*) Are the contents of this box one chessman or many chessmen?

There is no contradiction between saying that something, whether that something be the world or the contents of a box, is one, and saying that it is many. Contradiction would set in only if that something were said to be both one x and many x's. But in the original statement, whether about the world or about the chessmen, there was nothing about one x and many x's. That was foisted upon it by the critic. The contradiction of which the critic complains never existed in his victim's philosophy at all, until the critic planted it upon him, as he might have planted treasonable correspondence in his coat pockets; and with an equally laudable intention, to obtain a reward for denouncing him.

Thus, if a given doctrine D is criticized as self-contradictory because it is divisible into two parts E and F, where E contradicts F, the criticism is valid only if the critic has correctly reconstructed the questions to which E and F were given as answers. A critic who is aware of this condition will of course 'show his working' by stating to his readers the evidence on which he has concluded that the author criticized really did formulate his questions in such a way that E and F in his mouth were mutually contradictory. Failing that, a reader disinclined to work the problem out for himself will naturally assume the criticism to be sound or unsound according as he has found the critic to be, in a general way, a good historian or a bad one.

This enabled me to answer the question, left open in 1914, whether the 'realists'' critical methods were sound. The answer could only be that they were not. For the 'realists'' chief, and in the last resort, it seemed to me, only method was to analyse the position criticized into various propositions, and detect contradictions between these. Following as they did the rules of propositional logic, it never occurred to them that those contradictions might be the fruit of their own historical errors as to the questions which their victims had been trying to answer. There was also a chance that they might not be; but, after what I already knew about the 'realists'' attitude towards history, the odds seemed to me against it. In any case, so long as the possibility existed, the methods were vicious.

All this, during my spare time in 1917, I wrote out at considerable length, with a great many applications and illustrations, in a book called *Truth and Contradiction*. I went so far as to offer it to a publisher, but was told that the times were hopelessly bad for a book of that kind, and that I had better keep it for the present. The publisher was right on both points. Not only were the times unpropitious, but I was still a beginner in the art of writing books. I had only published one. It was called *Religion and Philosophy*, and was published in 1916. It had been written some years earlier, in order to tidy up and put behind me a number of thoughts arising out of my juvenile studies in theology; and I published it because, at a time when a young man's expectation of life was a rapidly dwindling asset, I wished at any rate to leave one philosophical publication behind me, and hated (as I still hate) leaving a decision of that kind to executors.

2. *The textual criticism of English classics**

In the *Proposals for Printing the Dramatick Works of William Shakespeare* Johnson wrote: 'To have a text corrupt in many places, and in many doubtful, is, among the authors that have written since the use of types, almost peculiar to *Shakespeare*. Most writers, by publishing their own works, prevent all various readings, and preclude all conjectural criticism.' Modern research has shown that books published by their authors are yet not immune from corruption; that Johnson himself knew this is shown by his practice. When they were in Skye, Johnson handed Boswell the works of Sir George Mackenzie, and bade him discover an error in the text on the sixty-fifth page of the first volume. 'I was lucky enough to hit it at once. As the passage is printed, it is said that the devil answers *even* in *engines*. I corrected it to *ever* in *aenigmas*. "Sir (said he), you are a good critick. This would have been a great thing to do in the text of an ancient authour." '

The causes to which it is due that the text of Shakespeare is less certain than that of Sophocles are well known. They have, perhaps, never been better stated than by Johnson:

Of the works of Shakespeare the condition has been far different; he sold them, not to be printed, but to be played. They were immediately copied for the actors, and multiplied by transcript

* From *The Portrait of a Scholar and Other Essays Written in Macedonia 1916–1918* by R. W. Chapman (London: Oxford University Press, 1922), pp. 65–79.

after transcript, vitiated by the blunders of the penman, or changed by the affectation of the player . . .; and printed at last without the concurrence of the author, without the consent of the proprietor, from compilations made by chance or by stealth out of the separate parts written for the theatre; and thus thrust into the world surreptitiously and hastily, they suffered another depravation from the ignorance and negligence of the printers, as every man who knows the state of the press in that age will readily conceive.

Shakespeare's text seemed to the critics of the eighteenth century to be peculiar only from their neglect of his contemporaries. Most of his fellow-dramatists were in a similar plight. Ben Jonson indeed saved his text from mutilation by himself preparing it for the press and by superintending the printing with laborious diligence; but his was a quite exceptional carefulness. Even writers who, unlike the dramatists, were at liberty to publish their works as soon as they were written, often preferred to circulate them in manuscript. Sidney had nothing to do with the printing of *Arcadia*; the publication of *The Passionate Pilgrim* was piratical; very few of Donne's poems were printed in his lifetime. Even those authors who deliberately published their works were at the mercy of printers to whom the method and regularity of the modern press were unknown. No proof was sent to the author. Mistakes were corrected, and fresh mistakes made, while the sheets were at the press. It is doubtful if any two copies of the First Folio are identical.

Conjectural emendation is not the first, but the last, duty of an editor; the first is to assemble and weigh the evidence. What Pope called 'the dull duty of an editor' has been greatly extended by modern diligence, which has found that copies of the same edition do not agree, and that varying texts abound in contemporary manuscript-books. As the accuracy of printing increased, and authors discovered a conscience, texts became less uncertain and an editor's path less perplexed; but variation and error persist. Editors of Gray and Keats must consult the manuscripts; editors of Wordsworth and Shelley must compare numerous editions.

It is generally accepted that the most authoritative edition is the last published in the author's lifetime. This is roughly true of books published in the last two centuries; but what if the author revised only the first edition, or revised no edition? Of the five editions of *The Shepheard's Calender*, each repeats the errors of its predecessors, and adds new errors of its own. Of the Shakespeare Folios, Johnson says, 'whoever has any . . . has all, excepting those diversities which mere reiteration of editions will produce'. The second edition of *The Faery Queene* contains changes which were certainly made by Spenser; but the 'faults escaped in the printing', of which a list was printed in 1590, were repeated in 1596. Even the careful Boswell, with Malone to help him, allowed errors to appear in the third edition 'revised and corrected' of his *Tour to the Hebrides* from which the first is free. It is therefore never admissible to select one edition and neglect the rest, unless the edition judged to be authoritative is the first.

Sometimes editions differ so widely that the constitution of an eclectic text becomes difficult, if not impossible. The Vulgate Shakespeare has been compiled from Quartos and Folio partly by selection, partly by conflation; and combines versions of the same scene, both of which may be Shakespearian, but which Shakespeare could never have intended to stand together. From such a problem some critics seek refuge by selecting one original and editing it as if it were unique. This is legitimate, but does not exhaust the duties of criticism. A Quarto and the Folio may give versions which, as a whole, it is impossible to reconcile or combine; yet if they contain passages substantially the same, the variations must be weighed. There is in Shakespeare a long sentence, which in the Folio is concluded by the words 'and in one purpose'. The text is defensible, though the sentence lacks a verb. The Quarto has 'end in one purpose'. It is now an editor's business to decide, not whether the Folio text is possible, but whether 'and' or 'end' is the more likely to be right. That Shakespeare wrote both at different times is possible—all things are possible—but is not probable; that a printer should confuse 'and' and 'end' is what happens on every page.

Donne is another author whose editors may be tempted to fly to this unitarian heresy. Most of his poems depend mainly upon the posthumous edition of 1633; but there are also many earlier manuscripts, of inferior authority as a whole (they are not the poet's autograph); and the later editions, which, as they include new poems, are not mere reprints, present variants which do not always seem due either to negligence or to conjecture. Such readings must be considered when the edition of 1633 is corrupt or doubtful, as it often is. To take one edition and ignore the rest because that edition is the best is no more defensible than to use one manuscript only of an ancient author because it is in general the most faithful. Yet since Donne is a poet not only obscure but often wantonly perverse, the decision whether specious variations come from a good manuscript source or from the ingenuity or negligence of an editor or printer will be always doubtful, and sometimes impossible. The text of 1633 we know to have been copied, however ill, from a good manuscript. The tendency to prefer the later and easier reading has given currency to versions which are not Donne, but Donne made smooth.

Boswell's *Journal of a Tour to the Hebrides* was carefully corrected by the author for the second and third editions. The third is the edition which he himself cites in the *Life of Johnson*, and it is obviously authoritative. Dr Birkbeck Hill accordingly discarded the first and second editions; and in one place corrected a misprint by conjecture which he might have corrected by reference to the first edition. This is a vicious principle. When the variations between the first and third editions are examined in detail, it is found that, though a great majority of the changes are clearly Boswell's, some are certainly the printer's, and a few are doubtful. Johnson 'was very severe on a lady, whose name was mentioned. He said he would have her sent to St Kilda.' (The reference was to another lady who actually had been marooned on St Kilda, and who had been talked of the day before.) The third edition has 'would have sent her'. This is less probable in itself, and it is most unlikely that Boswell made the change. In another place the first edition has 'will be pleased', the second 'will be please', the third 'will please'. Our unitarians are here committed to the view that it is more probable that Boswell altered 'be pleased' to 'please' than that the printer of the third edition, finding 'be please' in his copy, corrected it by omitting 'be'. 'Of these trifles enough.'

The works of later writers were published under more favourable conditions than were Shakespeare's or Donne's, and leave less room for conjecture; but conjecture is never inadmissible, and emendations may sometimes be probable. Johnson's rule 'always to turn the old text on every side, and try if there be any interstice, through which light can find its way', is sound; and in a writer 'so licentious as Shakespeare' few emendations can ever be considered certain. Less irregular writers, though their text may be less corrupt, may sometimes be corrected with greater confidence. That the text should stand, if it can be made to yield a meaning, is not always true. In Johnson's *Journey to the Western Islands* is this sentence: 'To disarm part of the Highlands, could give no reasonable occasion of complaint. Every Government must be allowed the power of taking away the treason that is lifted against it.' It cannot be said to be impossible that Johnson wrote this; but when it is considered that the expression is awkward, and therefore not Johnsonian; that the book contains some dozen palpable errors, all obviously due to a misreading of the manuscript which the author did not detect; and that 'treaſon' in Johnson's handwriting is very close to 'weapon'—it becomes more probable that the text is wrong than that it is right.[1] In the same book we read: 'Voluntary solitude was the great art of propitiation, by which crimes were effaced and conscience was appeased.' Other writers might call solitude an art, but hardly Johnson; 'act of propitiation' is a known

[1] The writer had before him a copy of the first edition which lacked the *Errata*. This correction is there anticipated.

formula, and the confusion of *r* and *c* was exceedingly common.[1] Even in the eighteenth and nineteenth centuries literature has been produced in conditions favourable to corruption. When Johnson wrote his *Rambler* the printer's devil was at the door and took the copy away as it was written. The present writer knows nothing of the text of the *Rambler*, except that in all editions 'temerity' for 'timidity', or 'timidity' for 'temerity', has made nonsense of one of Johnson's periods; but he should expect to find the original issue, at least, not free from error.

The most satisfactory emendation, though not the most gratifying to its author, is that in which not a letter is changed. Such is the ὄν καὶ μὴ ὄν which Bullen disinterred from 'oncaimion' (or some such Roman gibberish) in *Faustus*; the later editions made it 'œconomy'. Such is Macaulay's restoration to grammar of the first page of *Persuasion* by the alteration of a comma.

The present writer claims to have restored dramatic propriety to a place in *Pride and Prejudice*. In the second chapter the words 'When is your next ball to be, Lizzy?' appear at the end of a sentence spoken by Kitty Bennet. It is absurdly improbable that Kitty should be in need of such information. But her father, who had spoken just before, doubtless was ignorant of the date, and he had a reason for wanting to know. The speech can be given to him by a change which is hardly a change; for the word 'when' begins a line, and will begin a new speech if it is shifted to the right by a fraction of an inch.

> Were it not better done, as others use,
> To sport with Amaryllis in the shade
> Or with the tangles of Neaera's hair?

As these lines are commonly read, there is an awkwardness (pedantically called a zeugma) in the collocation of 'sport with Amaryllis' and 'sport with the tangles'; neither 'sport' nor 'with'

---

[1] In Johnson's note on *Henry V*, III. v. 40, it is said that a catalogue of misspelt French names is unaltered 'since the sense of the author is not affected'. Read 'affected'.

has quite the same shade of meaning in the two phrases. If 'with' be read to rhyme with 'scythe' (it is not necessary to write it 'withe') both sense and metre are improved.

The writer cannot refrain from quoting an *aperçu* of a learned friend, which is, he believes, still unpublished. There is a line in Marlowe, 'Our Pythagoras' Metempsychosis', which seems unmetrical. By supposing Marlowe to have pronounced Greek as it is pronounced in Greece today, and was often pronounced then, this critic produces a 'mighty line':

Our Pythagóras' Metempsýchosis.

Emendations more temerarious than these will sometimes occur. Sweeping changes are not often worth hazarding, because in books printed when they were first written it is unlikely that the text of the first edition has been corrupted more than once. But in editing Shakespeare and his contemporaries 'conjectural criticism', says Johnson, 'demands more than humanity possesses'. Yet 'the peril must not be avoided, nor the difficulty refused'.

The credibility of an emendation must be judged by estimating the probability of the corruption assumed as well as the propriety of the change proposed. Sir Walter Raleigh somewhere says that the change from 'way of life' to 'may of life' 'makes Shakespeare write like Pope'. But is there anything very unlike Shakespeare in 'my *May* of life'? Sir Walter rightly holds that in Shakespeare anything that has a meaning should not be lightly changed. But when it is remembered that an italic *m* inverted is very like a *w*, and that turned letters are very common, the probability of the corruption is so great, and the change so slight, that the emendation deserves consideration. If it is bad in itself, *cadit quaestio*. It is *a priori* probable that corruptions exist in Shakespeare which have never been and will never be suspected, because the lost word has been supplanted by another which makes sense. There is nothing improbable about 'Vaulting ambition which o'erleaps itself'. But when once 'sell' has been suggested, and the probability that 'sell' would be altered to 'self' is considered, it becomes difficult to be sure that 'self' is right. The late Professor Bywater used to say, 'I wish *I* had made that emendation.'

The practice of conjecture is pleasant, but like other pleasant things is dangerous. A commentator is apt to think that every line needs a note; Johnson said of Warburton that he 'had a rage for saying something when there was nothing to be said'. An emender is apt to acquire a rage for correcting when there is nothing to correct. Yet an editor is bound to satisfy himself that his text makes sense and grammar; and it is remarkable how the eye will mislead, and an inattentive mind acquiesce in imperfect meaning. Printers employ trained readers, because authors do not see small mistakes. They read the right word when the print has the wrong one. In reading Johnson's *Journey* the present aspirant three times missed the word 'reruined', because the catchword on the previous page had told him to expect 'required'. He would perhaps have acquiesced in 'treason' and 'art', if his vigilance had not been excited by 'thirteenth of August' when he knew from Boswell that it must be 'thirtieth'.

A useful and amusing exercise is to correct a reprint of a book, the most careless that can be found, and compare the emendations with a sound text. Vanity will sometimes be hurt; but sagacity will often be rewarded. The writer has seen the late Dr Verrall's copies of *Jane Austen* (modern reprint) and compared his marginal suggestions with the original editions. Some of them seemed to be unnecessary; of those which seemed probable, almost all were found to be the readings of the first edition.

The privilege of emendation has been too little exercised by modern editors of English classics; but it is true that emendation is only a small part of their duties. The chief is restoration. In this pious work Johnson was a pioneer. 'In this modest industry I have not been unsuccessful. I have rescued many lines from the violations of temerity.' The editors of the later Folios, and such men as Rowe, confounded emendation with what Johnson justly calls adulteration. They 'regulated' the text to suit their own views of propriety and elegance. In lesser matters they made changes as a matter of routine. When they altered 'Enter the two Bishops' to 'Enter the two Archbishops' (because they were Canterbury and York), and 'exit' to 'exeunt', when more than one person left the stage, they did not know they were doing wrong. A witty scholar commenting on this last piece of pedantry remarked, 'We do not say, Smith and Jones made an *affidaverunt*.' We now know the Folio, carelessly printed as it is, to be much better than Johnson supposed: 'I considered the punctuation as wholly in my power'; we now know that it is in the main sound. Johnson thought it permissible to 'smoothe the cadence, or regulate the measure' by transpositions and omissions from which we now shrink. Even the rearrangement of the lines to suit the blank verse has been called in question. There is a place in *Macbeth* where, in the Folio, the lines as printed do not scan; but the famous directions, 'Knock, Knock, Knock' are disposed on the page with such striking dramatic effect that it is hard to believe the arrangement accidental. What if it should follow Shakespeare's autograph?

The petulance and self-conceit of editors have in the past been notorious. The controversies of scholars are still sometimes more acrimonious than the dignity of their subject should warrant. But the editor of today is of necessity a humbler person than his predecessors. In the criticism and exegesis of modern, and even of ancient, literature, most of the obscurities that admit of enlightenment, and most of the corruptions that admit of correction, have been explained or mended. There is still room for labour, but not much room for fame. Yet the diligence of editors is still deserving of respect. To restore, and maintain in its integrity, the text of our great writers is a pious duty, and it is a surprisingly difficult task. An editor's business is to arrive at the truth, or as near it as he can; and to do this it is often necessary to spend time and labour on very small matters. 'To an editor,' says Johnson, 'nothing is a trifle by which his authour is obscured.' It is often his misfortune that he cannot but seem to come between his author and the reader's enjoyment, by labouring on 'evanescent atoms'. Because he seems to magnify atoms he is not to be supposed unaware of their insignificance. It is true that good judges of literature often make very bad editors; but it is unfair to conclude that an editor who knows his business, and sticks to it, is insensible of higher matters. On this, as on so many topics of criticism, the 'Preface to Shakespeare' has the last word:

> The greater part of readers, instead of blaming us for passing trifles, will wonder that on mere trifles so much labour is expended, with such importance of debate, and such solemnity of diction. To these I answer with confidence, that they are judging of an art which they do not understand; yet cannot much reproach them with their ignorance, nor promise that they would become in general, by learning criticism, more useful, happier, or wiser.

Y4 (SMOL HILL).
July 1918

3. *The wanderings and homes of manuscripts** *

The Wanderings and Homes of Manuscripts is the title of this book. To have called it the survival and transmission of ancient literature would have been pretentious, but not wholly untruthful. Manuscripts, we all know, are the chief means by which the records and imaginings of twenty centuries have been preserved. It is my purpose to tell where manuscripts were made, and how and in what centres they have been collected, and, incidentally, to suggest some helps for tracing out their history. Naturally the few pages into which the story has to be packed will not give room for any one episode to be treated exhaustively. Enough if I succeed in rousing curiosity and setting some student to work in a field in which an immense amount still remains to be discovered.

In treating of so large a subject as this—for it is a large one—it is not a bad plan to begin with the particular and get gradually to the general.

Some Specimen Pedigrees of MSS

I take my stand before the moderate-sized bookcase which contains the collection of MSS belonging to the College of Eton, and with due care draw from the shelves a few of the books

* From *The Wanderings and Homes of Manuscripts* by M. R. James, *Provost of Eton* (London: Society for Promoting Christian Knowledge, 1919), pp. 3–11, 33–47, 58–68.

which have reposed there since the room was built in 1729.

The first shelf I lay hands upon contains some ten large folios. Four of them are a single great compilation, beginning with a survey of the history of the world and of the Roman Empire, and merging into the heraldry of the German *noblesse*. It was made, we find, in 1541, and is dedicated to Henry VIII. Large folding pictures on vellum and portraits of all the Roman Emperors adorn the first volume. It is a sumptuous book, supposed to be a present from the Emperor Ferdinand to the King. How did it come here? A printed label tells us that it was given to the college by Henry Temple, Viscount Palmerston, in 1750 (he had previously given it to Sir Richard Ellys on whose death Lady Ellys returned it: so much in parenthesis). Then, more by luck than anything else, I find mention of it in the diary of Thomas Hearne, the Oxford antiquary; his friend Thomas Jett, F.R.S., owned it and told him about it in 1722: he had been offered £100 a volume for it; it was his by purchase from one Mr Stebbing. It was sold, perhaps to Palmerston, at Jett's auction in 1731. The gap between Henry VIII and Stebbing remains for the present unfilled. So much for the first draw.

Next, a yet larger and more ponderous volume, *Decreta Romanorum Pontificum*—the Papal decretals and the Acts of the Councils. It is spotlessly clean and magnificently written in a hand of the early part of the twelfth century, a hand which very much resembles that in use at Christchurch, Canterbury. I am, indeed, tempted to call it a Canterbury book; only it bears none of the marks which it ought to have if it was ever in the library of the Cathedral Priory. Was it perhaps written there and sold or given to a daughter-house, or to some abbey which had a less skilful school of writers? Not to Rochester, at any rate, though Rochester did get many books written at Christchurch. If it had belonged to Rochester there would have been some trace, I think, of an inscription on the lower margin of the first leaf. No; the only clue to the history is a title written on the fly-leaf in the fifteenth century, which says: 'The book of the decrees of the

Pope of Rome, and it begins on the second leaf "*tes viii*".' That does not tell us much; I do not recognize the handwriting of the title, though I guess it to have been written when the book came to Eton College. All I can say is that here is an example of a large class, duplicates of indispensable and common works, which the abbey libraries possessed in great numbers, and often parted with, in the fourteenth and fifteenth centuries, to colleges and private purchasers.

Next we take out a thin folio written on paper. This time it is a Greek book which we open; it has the works of the Christian apologists Athenagoras and Tatian, and a spurious epistle of Justin Martyr, copied in 1534 by Valeriano of Forlí. A single MS now at Paris, written in 914, is the ancestor of all our copies of these texts; but it has been shown that this Eton book is not an immediate copy of that, but of one now at Bologna. Obviously it was written in Italy. How does it come to be here? Sir Henry Wotton, Provost of the college, spent the best part of twenty years in Italy, mainly as Ambassador to the Court of Venice for James I, and left all his MSS to the college at his death in 1639. There are numbers of MSS from Italy in this bookcase, and, though hardly any of them have Wotton's name in them, it is not to be doubted that they came from him. A good proportion of them, too, can be traced back a step farther, for they have in them the name or the arms or the handwriting of Bernardo Bembo of Venice, the father of the more famous Cardinal Pietro Bembo. This Justin volume is not of that number, but we have a clue to its history which may be deemed sufficient.

I turn to another shelf and open a large book written somewhere about the year 1150, which was given to the college in 1713 by one of the Fellows; in 1594 it belonged to John Rogers (if I read the name right). It contains St Jerome's Commentary on Daniel and the Minor Prophets, followed by a tract of St Ambrose, and another ascribed to Jerome (subject, the hardening of Pharaoh's heart), which was in reality, we are now told, written by a Pelagian. It is a very uncommon text. After that we have Jerome's (so-called) prophecy of the fifteen signs which are to precede the last judgement—of which signs, let it be said in passing, there is a fine representation in an ancient window in the Church of All Saints, North Street, at York. Can we trace this volume any farther back than 1594? I think so; the Ambrose and the two spurious tracts of Jerome (one, as I said, being of very rare occurrence) are entered, in that order, in the catalogue of the library of Peterborough Abbey. The library has long been dispersed, but the catalogue remains, and was printed by Gunton in his History of the Abbey. But the said catalogue makes no mention of the Commentary of Jerome, which fills 323 out of the 358 leaves of our book. A serious obstacle, it will be said, to an identification; yet a long series of observations, too long to be set out here, has led me to the conclusion that our Peterborough catalogue makes a practice of not entering the main contents of the volumes, but only the short subsidiary tracts, which might else escape notice. And without much hesitation I put down the book before me as a relic of the Peterborough Library.

Somewhat higher up stands a very stout book bound in old patterned paper. The material of it is paper too, the language is Greek, and the contents, for the most part, Canons of Councils. There are two hands in it; one is perhaps of the fourteenth century, the other is of the early part of the fifteenth. This latter is the writing of one Michael Doukas, who tells us that he was employed as a scribe by Brother John of Ragusa, who held some position at a Church Council, unnamed. There were two Johns of Ragusa, it seems, both Dominicans, one of whom figured at the Council of Constance in 1413, the other at that of Basle in 1433. The latter must be the right one, for there are still Greek MSS at Basle which belonged to the Dominicans of that city, and were bequeathed by the second John at his death in 1442.

The book is important, because the first thing in it is the only copy of a treatise ascribed to St Athanasius, called a Synopsis of Holy Scripture. This treatise was printed first in 1600 by an editor named Felckmann, and no MS of it has been used or known since.

Where did Felckmann find it? In a MS which belonged to Pierre Nevelet, procured for him (the editor) by Bongars, a distinguished scholar of Orleans. Now, the Eton book has in it a whole series of names of owners, some erased, but decipherable. The earliest seems to be Joannes Gastius, who in 1550 gave it to Johannes Hernogius (as I doubtfully read it). Then come Petrus Neveletus and his son, I(saac) N(icolas) Neveletus. Evidently, then, we have here the MS which Felckmann used, and we arrive at some date after 1600. In 1665 or 1685 Daniel Mauclerc, Doctor of Law, living at Vitry le François, is the owner. He leaves France (the family were Huguenots), and brings the book to Holland. His son Jacques, Doctor of Medicine, has it in 1700, in England; his nephew, John Henry Mauclerc, also M.D., succeeds to it and enters his name in 1748, and gives it to Mr Roger Huggett, Conduct and Librarian of the College, who died in 1769.

This is an unusually full and clear pedigree. One more, and I have done.

This time it is a copy of the Polychronicon of Ranulph Higden, monk of Chester; it was the popular history of the world and of England for anyone who could read Latin in the fifteenth century. No abbey library could be without it, just as no gentleman's library could be without a copy of the English Chronicle called the Brut. Here is a case in which we know the beginning and end of the book's wanderings, but not the middle of the story. The arms of Eton adorn the beginning of each of the seven 'books' of the Chronicle, so we may take it that it was owned from the first by a member of the foundation. An inscription tells us that within the fifteenth century it belonged to the Carthusians of Witham in Somerset, and was given to them by Master John Blacman. Here is light. John Blacman was Fellow and Chanter of Eton, then Head of a House (King's Hall) in Cambridge, and lastly a Carthusian monk. He was also confessor to Henry VI, and wrote a book about him. In a MS at Oxford there is a list of the books he gave to Witham, and among them is this Polychronicon. More: he has prefixed to the text a pedigree of the Kings of England from

Egbert, illustrated with drawings, the last of which is the earliest known representation of Windsor Castle. We have not, then, to complain of lack of information about the early stages of the history; but then comes a gap, and between the Dissolution and the early part of the nineteenth century, when Rodd of London had it and sold it to the fourth Earl of Ashburnham, I can (at present) hear nothing of the book. In quite recent years it passed from the Ashburnham family to Mr H. Y. Thompson, from him to Mr George Dunn, and at his death was bought back for its first home.

There, then, are half a dozen histories of MSS, fairly typical and fairly diverse. Naturally I have picked out books which have some traceable story. Very many have none. We can only say of them that they were written in such a century and such a country, and acquired at such a date: and there an end. Rebinding and loss of leaves, especially of fly-leaves, have carried off names of owners and library-marks, and apart from that there are but very few cases in which we are warranted in proclaiming from the aspect and character of the script that a book was written at one particular place and nowhere else.

I think it will be seen, from what has been said, that my subject is one which depends for its actuality upon the accumulation of a great number of small facts. There is, of course, a broad historical background: no less than the whole history of Western Europe since the period of the Barbarian invasions. That cannot be looked for here, of course; but there are certain *data* of capital importance which cannot be spared, and some plotting out of the whole field is indispensable.

The Limits of the Subject

Greek and Latin MSS are the main subject. Oriental books we do not even touch upon, and vernacular books in English or French have to take a secondary place; and we may treat first of the Greek, for it is by far the most compact division. In the case of both Greek and Latin books we shall ask where and when they were chiefly made, when and how they left their early homes, and where they are to be found now.

Chronological Survey

Since this little book is not a treatise on palæography, a manual of art, or a history of learning, and yet has to touch upon all three provinces, it is important to keep it from straying too far into any of them, and this is one of the most difficult tasks that I have ever enterprised. The temptation to dilate upon the beauty and intrinsic interest of the MSS and upon the characteristic scripts of different ages and countries is hard to resist. And, indeed, without some slight elucidation of such matters my readers may be very much at fault.

I had begun a geographical survey of the field, taking countries as the units, and had written upon Italy and Spain, and attempted France. But I found that when the thirteenth and fourteenth centuries were reached my tract was becoming a disquisition upon palæography, art, and learning, and, of course, was failing to do justice either to any one of them or to what it had promised in its title. I now think that a chronological survey will be more practicable, and that it will be best to take first the subject of book-production, looking at each country in turn in a single period, instead of following the course taken by each, from the sixth century to the fifteenth.

Sixth and Seventh Centuries. Italy, France, and Spain are the main centres. Ireland is active in learning, and in the second half of the seventh century England, under Archbishop Theodore and Abbot Hadrian, produces schools which rival the Irish, and, in the person of Bede, has the greatest scholar of the time. Some of the great Irish monasteries, such as Bobbio, Luxeuil, St Gall, are founded on the Continent.

Books are produced in considerable numbers in Italy, France, Spain; and from Italy they are exported, especially by English pilgrims, such as Benedict Biscop. The Gospel harmony written in 546 by or for Bishop Victor of Capua comes to England, and goes abroad again, with St Boniface, perhaps, and now rests at Fulda, where also his body lies. A copy of St Jerome on Ecclesiastes, written in Italy in the sixth or seventh century, has in it the Anglo-Saxon inscription, 'The book of Cuthsuuitha the Abbess'. The only Abbess Cuthsuuitha we know of presided over a nunnery in or near Worcester about 690–700. Her book travelled to Germany with some British or English missionary, and is at Würzburg. Würzburg is an Irish foundation; its apostle and patron, St Kilian, is said to have been assassinated in 689. From Italy, too, came (most likely) the illustrated Gospels now at Corpus Christi College, Cambridge (286), which belonged once to Christchurch, Canterbury; and the beautiful little copy of St John's Gospel at Stonyhurst College, which was found in the coffin of St Cuthbert (d. 687) when it was opened in 1104. And St Gall must have acquired its ancient Virgil from Italy also—when, we do not know.

Spain kept her books very much to herself, one would guess, judging from the very few Spanish MSS of this age which are to be met with in the rest of Europe. The guess, however, would not be quite correct. There was one great Spanish scholar in the seventh century, Isidore of Seville (636), and his encyclopædia (The *Etymologies* or *Origins*), which fed many later centuries with learning, made its way all over educated Europe very quickly. Not only so, but we find English scholars (Aldhelm and Bede) quoting Spanish writers on grammar and Spanish poets who were almost their own contemporaries.

Eighth Century. This sees the last part of Bede's career (d. 734)—the zenith of English scholarship, the mission of St Boniface (d. 758) to Germany, the meeting of Alcuin with Charlemagne (781), and the beginning of the Carolingian Renaissance. But, on the other hand, Spain is overrun by the Moors, Italy is inert, England begins to be harried by the Northmen. On the whole, if there really was a Dark Age, the middle of the eighth century seems to answer the description best. But, of course, there were points of light. The great centres of Northern France, such as Corbie and Laon, particularly Corbie, were beginning their activities of collecting and copying books. Ireland was capable of producing such a work as the Book of Kells—whether it actually falls within the century or not I will not be positive, but work of the same amazing beauty was carried out before 800. Nor was the export of treasures from Italy to England quite stopped, in spite of difficulties. At the Plantin Museum at Antwerp is a copy of the writings of the Christian poet Sedulius, which has pictures of the old Italian sort, such as we find in the frescoes of the Roman catacombs. In it is a note connecting it with a Bishop of the name of Cuthwin, who held the East Anglian see and died about 754. Another MS, at Paris, has a note describing an elaborately illustrated life of St Paul, which, it says, the same Bishop Cuthwin brought with him from Rome.

Ninth Century. There is immense activity, literary and artistic, afoot at the Court of Charlemagne (d. 814) and of his successors. The German abbeys—e.g. Lorsch, Fulda—and cathedral schools (Mainz, Bamberg, etc.) are full of scribes and teachers. Irishmen who know Greek flock to the Continent, driven from home by Danish invasion: such are Johannes Scottus Eriugena and Sedulius Scottus. They haunt Liége, Laon, Aix-la-Chapelle, and penetrate to Italy. Not less prolific are the French houses: at Tours the handwriting called the Carolingian minuscule, the parent of our modern 'Roman' printing, is developed, though not at Tours alone. At Corbie, Fleury on the Loire (now called St Bénoit sur Loire), St Riquier by Abbeville, Rheims, and many another centre in Northern and Eastern France, libraries are accumulated and ancient books copied. Of St Gall and Reichenau the same may be said. In Italy, Verona is conspicuous. The archdeacon Pacificus (d. 846) gave over 200 books to the cathedral, where many of them still are; and at Monte Cassino, the head house of the Benedictine Order, books were written in the difficult 'Beneventane' hand (which used to be called Lombardic, and was never popular outside Italy). Spain has its own special script at this time, the

Visigothic, as troublesome to read as the Beneventane; its *a*'s are like *u*'s and its *t*'s like *a*'s. England is still overrun by the Danes, and does nothing before the very end of the century, when King Alfred exerts himself to revive education, and starts a vernacular literature.

An enormous proportion of the earliest copies we have of classical Latin authors come from this century, when old copies of them were actively sought out and transcribed. Often great liberties in the way of revision and even abridgment of the text were taken by the scholars of the time, and, once transcribed, the old archetypes were neglected or even destroyed.

Books of very great beauty—Bibles, Gospels, Psalters—were produced for the Emperors and the great nobles and prelates. In these there is a marked effort to imitate and continue the traditions of classical art.

Tenth Century. The tradition of study and scholarship lives on, but the impulse from Britain and Ireland has worked itself out, and few geniuses are born on the Continent. There is a period of splendour and vigour in England under the Kings Athelstan and Edgar and the Archbishops Odo and Dunstan. The calligraphic school of Winchester achieves magnificent results. At the end of the century the great teacher and scholar Gerbert (Pope Sylvester II) is a prominent figure at the Imperial Court. The Ottos emulate Charlemagne in their zeal for literature and for fine works of art, but their attainment is slighter.

Eleventh Century. Men still live on the traditions of the Carolingian Revival in the early part: there is later an awakening, principally, perhaps, in France and Italy. Great names like those of Anselm, Abelard, Bernard, come forward. Monastic reform is active; great schools, as at Chartres, take their rise; there is a preparation for the wonderful vigour of the next century. The First Crusade brings East and West together in a new fashion.

Twelfth Century. The strength and energy of Europe is now tremendous in every department, and not least in that with which we are concerned. Our libraries are crammed today with twelfth-century MSS. The Gregories, Augustines, Jeromes, Anselms, are numbered by the hundred. It is the age of great Bibles and of 'glosses'—single books or groups of books of the Bible equipped with a marginal and interlinear comment (very many of which, by the way, seem to have been produced in North Italy). Immense, too, is the output of the writers of the time; Bernard, Hugh and Richard of St Victor, Peter Comestor, Peter Lombard. The two last are the authors of two of the most popular of medieval textbooks—Peter Lombard of the *Sentences* (a body of doctrine), Peter Comestor of the *Historia Scholastica* (a manual of Scripture history). The Cistercian Order, now founding houses everywhere, is, I think, especially active in filling its libraries with fine but austerely plain copies of standard works, eschewing figured decoration in its books, as in its buildings, and caring little for secular learning. The University of Paris is the centre of intellectual vigour.

Thirteenth Century. This is commonly regarded as the greatest of all in medieval history; and truly, when we think of achievements such as Westminster, Amiens, and Chartres, and of men such as St Louis, St Thomas Aquinas, St Francis, Dante, Edward I, Roger Bacon, we must agree that the popular estimate is sound. Certainly we see in France and in England the fine flower of art in buildings and in books.

Paris is still the centre. The 'Gothic' spirit is concentrated there. The book trade is enormous. It is passing—under the influence of the University, most likely—out of the hands of the monastic scribes into those of the professional 'stationers'; while great individual artists, such as Honoré, arise to provide for Royal and noble persons examples of art which stand as high today as when they were first produced.

It is now that we find a large multiplication of textbooks. If the twelfth century was the age of great Bibles, the thirteenth is the age of small ones. Thousands of these exist, written with amazing minuteness and uniformity. Only less common are the Aristotles, the *Sentences*, the *Summae*, and the other works of the golden age of scholasticism. The Orders of Friars, Franciscan and Dominican, form libraries—partly of duplicates procured from older foundations, partly of new copies to which they were helped by charitable friends.

Towards the end of the century Italy comes forward as the great purveyor of books of a special sort. The University of Bologna becomes the great law school of Europe, and exports in numbers copies of the immense texts and commentaries of and upon the Church (Canon) and Roman (Civil) law which were indispensable to the unfortunate student. These books become common at the end of the thirteenth century, and run over well into the fourteenth. They are prettily (but often very carelessly) written in a round Gothic hand, sometimes christened 'Bolognese'. Some were not only written but decorated (with poorish ornament) on the spot, but very many were exported in sheets and provided, in France or England, with such decoration as the purchaser could afford. A leading example is a copy of the Decretals in the British Museum (Royal 10, E. iv.) which belonged to St Bartholomew's, Smithfield. It is in Italian script, but on each of the spacious lower margins of its many pages is a picture by an English artist; these pictures run in sets, illustrating Bible stories, legends, and romances.

As the centuries go on, the material they have left increases in bulk, and the complication of the threads is proportionately greater. I cannot hope in a survey like this to give prominence to every factor; but we shall not be wrong in fixing upon Northern France and England as the areas of greatest productiveness and the sources of the best art in the thirteenth century.

Before we pass to the next century a word must be devoted to a not unimportant class of books which seem to have been manufactured chiefly in Picardy and Artois, the illustrated Romances—e.g. the Grail and Lancelot—of great bulk, usually in prose, which served to pass the winter evenings of persons of quality. A few of these, and a book of devotions to take to church (oftenest a Psalter at this time; later on a book of Hours), were the staple books owned by the upper classes.

Fourteenth Century. If the thirteenth century gives us on the whole the noblest books, the early part of the fourteenth affords the loveliest. They come from England, France, and the Netherlands. A noticeable element in their art is that of the grotesque and burlesque, never, of course, quite absent even from early books, but now most prominent and most delightful. The defect of the art of this time is lack of strength and austerity; its delicacy is above praise.

The middle of the century sees Petrarch, and with him the Renaissance begins. Italy has been producing great men in every field, but the work of Petrarch reached farther and was more enduring than that of any other.

France, tortured by wars, put forth little in the middle years, but then came Charles V, a King who was really interested in books, and the library he formed at the Louvre gave a stimulus to book-production which spread wide and lasted long. Under Richard II and through his Queen, Anne of Bohemia, a foreign influence makes itself felt in England, and some lovely results are achieved; but on the whole English art is waning.

The Universities, and to some extent the monasteries, were throughout this century great customers for the bulky books of scholastic divinity (Duns Scotus, Albertus, and the like) and the later generation of commentators on the Bible, such as Nicolas de Lyra and Hugo de S. Caro. Many shelves are filled with these.

Fifteenth Century. The fifteenth century is our last; it ends the MS period. Under the influence of the Renaissance, now enormously potent, every Italian noble forms a library. The scholars are seeking out the ninth-century copies of the classics, and they discard the Gothic (black-letter) hands of the thirteenth and fourteenth centuries in favour of the Carolingian minuscule (or, some say that of the twelfth century). As early as 1426 we find books written in a script adapted and refined from this; we call it a Roman hand, though the great centre of its propagation seems to have been Florence. In all essentials it is the parent of the type in which this page will be printed.

Italy, then, is the hub of the universe for books; and in Italy, Florence, Naples, and Rome are the most active *nuclei*. We have a record written by a Florentine bookseller, Vespasiano Bisticci, in the form of short biographies of great persons, many of whom had dealt with him. For some he provided whole libraries, as for Frederick, Duke of Urbino, whose books are now mostly in the Vatican. Such a man as this would not look at a printed book— which in Vespasiano's mind is, of course, very greatly to his credit; for the press was bound to put an end to his particular industry. We still find, by the way, this prejudice against print in the very last years of the century. Some rich persons had MS copies actually made from printed editions and elaborately illustrated. Such a one was Raphael de Marcatellis, natural son of Philip the Good of Burgundy and titular Bishop of Rhossus, near Antioch.[1] Part of his library may be found at Ghent, part at Holkham, and stray volumes at Cambridge (Peterhouse) and in the Arundel collection at the British Museum. They are very handsome books, and many have full-page paintings by capable artists, but the resulting impression is on the whole that of decadence.

Matthias Corvinus, King of Hungary (d. 1490), is a name famous among old bibliophiles. He got together a library of fine books, mostly recent copies made for him, and it was dispersed and sacked by the Turks in 1526. It is spoken of with bated breath by the old writers, as if it had contained priceless treasures. I am sceptical.

Ferdinand of Aragon and Calabria was a collector of the same kind, whose beautiful books, adorned with his arms in the lower margin of the first page, are many of them at Valencia, having passed to the University there by way of the Abbey of St Miguel de Los Reyes. These are of Italian and not of Spanish manufacture, and very fine they are.

These last-mentioned libraries have been scattered, but there are still some of the Renaissance period which survive in their

[1] See Eubel, *Hierarchia Catholica Medii Ævi*, ii. 248.

original homes. The Laurentian at Florence and the Vatican at Rome stand at the head of all. With regard to the latter it may be said that though earlier Popes, of course, had libraries (that of Avignon was quite considerable), yet Nicholas V (d. 1455) must be regarded as the founder of the Vatican library in its present state. So, too, the Marciana at Venice and the Malatestiana at Cesena must rank as genuine Renaissance collections.

It was not only the great men who loved to have books. The tribe of scholars, foreign as well as native, who coveted them was numerous. Every library now has its quota of humbler copies of the classics, often on paper, in the Roman or the more cursive Italic hand, not written by a professional scribe. Often these are of infinitesimal value, transcripts of extant copies of no greater age; but there is always the possibility that they may be a competent scholar's own careful apograph of some ancient MS which a Poggio had unearthed at St Gall, and which has since vanished. A glance at the *apparatus criticus* of a few editions of classics will show that often a fifteenth-century MS ranks high among the authorities for the text. Pedigree is what matters, not beauty of hand, nor, necessarily, date.

It has been the fate of these scholars' books, as it is the fate of all MSS, to be absorbed into great libraries, and many of them lurk there still unexamined and their origin undetermined. Discoveries, no doubt, yet remain to be made among them.

Whether or not a breath of influence from Italy was the cause, it is plain that library-making was popular in countries and circles which were not obviously affected by the Renaissance. The monasteries of England were certainly not so affected, yet we find many of them setting their books in order and building special rooms to contain them. Christchurch at Canterbury and Bury St Edmunds are leading instances. Now, too, universities and colleges made fresh catalogues, and received large accessions of books.

If the Renaissance did not touch the English public as a whole in this century, it made some proselytes. Among Englishmen who dealt with our Florentine Vespasiano were John Tiptoft, Earl of Worcester, Humphrey, Duke of Gloucester, William Gray, Bishop of Ely, Andrew Holes, of Wells. Others who resorted to Italy were John Free, Thomas Linacre, John Gunthorpe, Dean of Wells, William Flemming, Dean of Lincoln, William Tilley of Sellinge, Prior of Christchurch, Canterbury. We shall see later on what traces some of these have left on our libraries.

In places to which the Italian influence did not penetrate the humdrum trade of copying went on. Anselm, Bernard, and Augustine; sermon-books by the score; Burley on Aristotle, etc. Then, in another class, the production of books for use in church was very large. There were few Bibles, but Missals, Breviaries, large choir-books to be laid on the lectern, Graduals and Processionals, are legion. Then, again, every well-to-do person must have his or her Book of Hours, illuminated if possible. Such things were common wedding-presents, it seems. Upon the best of them really great artists were employed, like Foucquet of Tours and Gerard David; we even find Perugino painting a page in one, but the average are shop work made for the Italian market at Naples or Florence, for the French at Paris, Tours, Rouen, for the English very often at Bruges, where also many sumptuous chronicle books and French versions of secular history and romances were turned out. Edward IV had a considerable number of such in his library.

These private Prayer Books are, of course, incomparably the commonest of all illuminated manuscripts. They vary from loveliness to contemptibility. Perversely, they figure in catalogues, and are lettered on their backs, as Missals; our ancestors of the eighteenth and nineteenth centuries forgot that a Missal must contain the service of the Mass, and that none of these books do.

There, then, is a second survey of our ground, somewhat more detailed than the first, but woefully sketchy. Everyone who has studied MSS of any class or period would detect omissions in it which for him would vitiate the whole story. The best I can hope is that the assertions in it are not incorrect, and that it gives a true notion of the general course of book-production in medieval times.

Catalogues of MSS

We are best off if we have a catalogue of our abbey library, and preferably a late one; for in that case not only will the library be at its fullest, but probably the cataloguer will have set down, after the title of each book, the first words of its second leaf. Does this need explanation? Perhaps. In MSS, unlike printed books, the first words of the second leaf will be different in any two copies, say, of the Bible; the scribes did not make a page for page or line for line copy of their archetype—in fact, they may probably have avoided doing so purposely. By the help of such a catalogue we can search through collections of MSS, noting the second leaves in each case, and, it may be, identifying a considerable number of books. It is a laborious but an interesting process.

But, alas! such catalogues are very few; we have them for Durham, St Augustine's Abbey, Canterbury (and partly also for Christchurch), St Paul's Cathedral, Exeter Cathedral, Dover Priory, the Austin Friars of York (all now in print), and for not many more.

Next best it is to have a catalogue enumerating the contents of each volume; and next, and commonest, one which gives usually but a single title to each. Among the most useful I reckon those of Christchurch, Canterbury, Peterborough (an anomalous one), Glastonbury, Bury St Edmunds, Rochester, Dover, Lincoln, Leicester Abbey (not yet printed in full), Ramsey, Rievaulx, Lanthony-by-Gloucester, Titchfield. There are a good many short catalogues for smaller houses, written on the fly-leaves of books, which do not, as a rule, help us much. The list of monastic catalogues, however, is dreadfully defective. We have none for St Albans or Norwich or Crowland or Westminster, for Gloucester or Worcester, St Mary's, York, or Fountains. What do we do in such cases?

The Evidence of MSS Themselves

We have to depend, of course, on the evidence of the MSS themselves. It was happily a common practice to write on the fly-leaf or first leaf *Liber (Sancte Marie) de (tali loco)*. This is decisive. Then, again, some libraries devised a system of press-marks, such as 'N. lxviii', let us say. You find this in conjunction with the inscription of ownership; it is a Norwich book, you discover, that you have in hand, and all books showing press-marks of that form are consequently Norwich books too. Or you will find the name of a donor. 'This book was the gift of John Danyell, Prior.' Search in Dugdale's *Monasticon* will reveal, perhaps, that John Danyell was Prior of St Augustine's, Bristol, in 1459. A clue to locality will often be given in such a case by the monk's surname, for it was their custom to call themselves by the name of their native village. Thus, a monk named John Melford or William Livermere will be a Suffolk man, and the abbey in which he was professed is likely to be Bury. Coming to later times, it is apparent that at the Dissolution groups of books from a single abbey came into the hands of a single man. If I find Dakcombe on the fly-leaf of a MS, I am almost entitled to assume that it is a Winchester book: John Stonor got his books from Reading Abbey, John Young drew from Fountains, and so forth. Lastly, and most rarely, you are justified in saying that the handwriting and decoration of this or that book shows it to have been written at St Albans or at Canterbury. Hitherto the instances where this is possible are few, but I do not doubt that multiplication of observations will add to their number.

In questioning a MS for any of these indications (except the last) you must be on the look-out for signs of erasures, especially on the margins of the first leaf and on the fly-leaves at either end. Here the owner's name was usually written. Often it was accompanied by a curse on the wrongful possessor, and at the Dissolution there were many wrongful possessors, who, whether disliking the curse or anticipating trouble from possible buyers, thought it well to erase name, and curse, and all. They seldom did it so thoroughly that the surface of the vellum does not betray where it was, and it can be revived by the dabbing (*not* painting) upon it of ammonium bisulphide, which, unlike the old-fashioned galls, does not stain the page. Dabbed on the surface with a soft paint-brush, and dried off at once with clean blotting paper, it makes the old record leap to light, sometimes with astonishing clearness, sometimes slowly, so that the letters cannot be read till next day. It is not always successful; it is of no use to apply it to writing in red, and its smell is overpowering, but it is the elixir of palaeographers.

Yet, when all has been done, there is a sadly large percentage of MSS which preserve an obstinate silence. They have been re-bound (that is common), and have lost their fly-leaves in the process, or, worse than that, they have lain tossing about without a binding and their first and last quires have dropped away. In such cases we can only tell, from our previous experience in ancient handwritings, the date and country of their origin.

English Libraries

And now to turn to some individual libraries. Some of the most venerable have practically disappeared—that of Glastonbury, for instance, the premier abbey of England, the only one which lived through from British to Saxon times.[1] To it we might reasonably look to trace many an ancient book belonging to the days of the old British Church. Leland, who visited the library not long before the Dissolution, represents himself as overawed by its antiquity. But almost the only record he quotes is one by 'Melkinus', which most modern writers think was a late forgery. However, there is in the Bodleian one British book from Glastonbury, written, at

[1] We have its catalogue admirably reproduced by Thomas Hearne, at a time (early in the eighteenth century) when it was rare to find anyone who would take the trouble to make a faithful copy of such a record, with all its erasures and alterations.

least in part, in Cornwall, and preserving remnants of the learning of the British clergy. It has portions of Ovid and of Latin grammar, and passages of the Bible in Greek and Latin. The catalogue, too, shows that there were in fact a good number of old MSS, and also that the monks of the fourteenth century did not care much about them, for they are marked as 'Old and useless', 'Old and in bad condition' (*debilis*), and so on. The actual extant books which we can trace to this foundation are few and for the most part late.

St Albans, founded by King Offa in the eighth century, has left us, as I said, no catalogue, but there are many of its books in our libraries. Two groups of them stand out. First are those procured by Abbot Simon (1166–1188) and Prior Mathias. These are very finely written. A typical and very interesting specimen is a Bible at Eton (26) which has three columns to a page—a rare distinction in the twelfth century, pointing, perhaps, to its having been copied from a very early and venerable model. It has a sister book at Corpus Christi, Cambridge, and another—a New Testament—at Trinity College, Dublin. Then we have a large and important group of histories. The historiographers of St Albans form a series reaching from Roger of Wendover (d. 1236) to Thomas Walsingham (d. 1422). The greatest of them was Matthew Paris (d. 1259). We have authentic and even autograph copies of many of these works, and especially of Paris's (at Corpus Christi, Cambridge (26 and 16), and in the British Museum, Royal 14, C. vii., Cotton Nero D. 1, etc.). And we have not only Paris's writing, but many of his drawings, for he was an accomplished artist. All these books furnish us with material for judging of the hand-writing used at St Albans in the twelfth and thirteenth centuries, and we can speak with fair confidence of St Albans books of that period.

As in other cases, I believe that many books were written there for other monasteries, either as gifts or as a matter of business. Not every one of the little priories scattered all over the country had its own scriptorium; it was only natural that they should apply to the big establishments when they wanted a Bible or service-book or commentary of really good quality. This practice explains the fact that we quite often find books which we could make oath are products of St Albans or of Canterbury, and which yet have inscriptions, written when they were new books, showing that they were owned by some small house. Let me here note two other ways in which books wandered from the great abbeys. *One:* all the abbey libraries were full of duplicates; read any catalogue, and you will realize that. When the Orders of Friars were collecting libraries of their own, and when the colleges in the two Universities were doing the same, they found that the monks were often willing to part with one of their eight or nine sets of Gregory's *Moralia* or Augustine *On the Trinity* for a consideration. *Two:* most of the large abbeys maintained hostels at the Universities, singly or jointly, in which some of their younger members studied for degrees. These hostels were equipped with libraries, and the libraries were furnished from the shelves of the mother-houses. We have at least two lists of books so used: one of those which Durham sent to what is now Trinity College, Oxford; the other of those which Christchurch, Canterbury, deported to Canterbury College, Oxford, which stood on the site of Canterbury Quad, in Christ Church.

There was some compensation, by the way: the abbeys were not invariably the losers. A group of books (at Lambeth) was procured to be written by a Canon of Lanthony when he was studying at Oxford (about 1415), and given to the library of his priory.

We have digressed from the particular to the general. Returning to individual libraries, let us glance at the Norwich Cathedral Priory. Of this, again, we have no catalogue; it is a case in which press-marks and names of owners are our guides. Norwich has a system of press-marks consisting of a letter of the alphabet plus a Roman numeral: 'N. lxvii'. The press-marks of several other houses consist of just the same elements, but we can pick out that of Norwich by its size (not large) and its position (top of the first leaf of text); also there is usually added to it the name of the monk who procured it for the house, Henry de Lakenham or W. Catton—someone whose surname is the name of a Norfolk village. Over a hundred MSS from Norwich are known to me, but they are a very small fraction of the library, as is shown by the numerals attached to the several class letters. Very few of them are as old as the twelfth century; late twelfth and particularly early fourteenth make up the bulk. I attribute this to the great fire of 1286, and I take it that then the greater part of the priory books were spoiled, and that energetic steps to refill the library were taken in the years that followed. There are more Norwich books in the University Library at Cambridge than anywhere else; it has not been proved, but I do not much doubt, that most of them were given by the chapter to Cambridge about 1574, at the suggestion of Dr Andrew Perne, Master of Peterhouse, who was a member of the cathedral body and an enthusiast for the University Library.

Not very dissimilar was the action of Exeter Chapter, who in 1602 gave over eighty of their MSS to Sir Thomas Bodley's new library in Oxford, Bodley's brother being then a Canon of Exeter; and not long after the Canons of Worcester picked out a score of their MSS, for Dean Williams's new library at Westminster Abbey. These, however, I believe were never actually sent off. It is just as well, for the Westminster MSS were burnt in 1694. Of Bury St Edmunds I have attempted to write the history elsewhere, but it is not likely that many readers of this book will be familiar with my former publication. The only catalogue we have for this abbey is an early one (eleventh to twelfth century) written on the fly-leaves of a copy of Genesis (glossed) at Pembroke College, Cambridge. Thus it contains no fourteenth- or fifteenth-century books, nor, indeed, has it many entries of extant books of earlier date which we are sure belonged to Bury; but it is not to be despised, though we depend more upon press-marks than upon it for guidance. Bury press-marks were an introduction of the late fourteenth or early fifteenth century. Soon after 1400 Abbot Curteys built a library, and it was under the care of the monk, John Boston, who, I think, is responsible for the press-marks, as he certainly is for the copious bibliographical notices which occurred in some of the books. The press-marks consist of a capital letter and an *arabic* numeral (A. 130). Here, again, one has to be familiar with the handwriting of the marks and their position (top of first leaf and fly-leaf) in order to distinguish them from those of Exeter (often on last fly-leaf and large) or of the Hereford Franciscans (large, on first fly-leaf). However, in most cases they are backed up by the older inscription *Liber S. Ædmundi regis et martiris*. Bury library has, on the whole, fared well; an Alderman of Ipswich, William Smart, procured over 100 of its MSS, which he gave to Pembroke College, Cambridge, in 1599, and about 150 others are scattered up and down the country. One Bury book of extreme interest— not a library book, but a register—was taken across the Channel in the sixteenth century by a Bury monk to the settlement of the Benedictine refugees at Douai. Since the Revolution it has been (*perhaps* still is) in the town library there. Its importance is that it contains a list of the benefactors of the abbey, and among other things records the burial-places of the Abbots, including the famous Samson. In recent years it has guided excavators to the discovery of his bones. With it is a Psalter of extraordinary beauty, one of a group of marvellous books done in East Anglia— some say at Gorleston—soon after 1300. I grieve to hear that it has been severely damaged by damp. It has in it the name of an Abbot, John, who, I wish to believe, was of Bury, but doubt is thrown on this.

Seymour de Ricci

4. *English collectors**

The subject of these lectures may seem trifling and even irrelevant. If I had attempted to draw a sketch of the history of book-collecting in England from the year 1530, or even to condense in as few words as possible the biography of England's more notable bibliophiles, the object of my labours would possibly appear as more clearly intelligible. But why concentrate our efforts on marks of ownership? Why tackle a most interesting bibliographical problem—the history and causes of the variations of taste in book-collecting—by one of its smallest and most insignificant aspects? Why lose sight of the broader aspects of science for the sake of apparently unworthy minutiae? A recent experience—if I may be allowed to bring in personal reminiscences —will, I hope, make clear my plan and explain my intentions.

A few months ago, a distinguished American scholar, writing a book on the library of one of Petrarch's contemporaries, the humanist Coluccio Salutati, called on me in Paris and asked me if I could help him to trace any unrecorded books annotated by the learned fourteenth-century scholar. I gave him what scanty information my library and bibliographical notes enabled me to supply and he was about to leave my rooms, when he added quite casually: 'If by any chance you happen to run across one of Coluccio's books, you can in many cases tell it straight away, by

* From *English Collectors of Books and Manuscripts 1530–1930* (Cambridge: University Press, 1930), chapter 1.

the presence on the first page, in the upper right-hand corner, of two numerals separated by the word *carte* [leaves] in a small and neat semi-gothic hand.'

As he spoke, I seemed to focus gradually in my memory the distinct vision of a manuscript in my own library. I went to a book-case in the next room and took down from the shelves a manuscript of Florus, with the tell-tale inscription on the title-page and with numerous early marginal notes, a certain number of which my American visitor immediately recognized to be unquestionably in the hand of Coluccio Salutati. The careful notice which this scholar had taken of an apparently insignificant detail had thus enabled him to add to his store some new material of scientific importance.

Over a century ago, Horace Walpole wittily insisted that the pedigree of a work of art was certainly on a par with that of a race-horse. Books and manuscripts have likewise pedigrees, and in many cases the establishment of these pedigrees is founded on the study of hardly noticeable marks of ownership. Is it not time that some kind of an attempt should be made to set these marks down in print and even to reproduce in facsimile those which may seem to present the greatest general interest?

To the uninitiated, one manuscript seems very much like another manuscript: one old book resembles greatly any other copy of the same old book. The constant handling of printed and written material awakens gradually the eye to subtle differences between individual books and manuscripts. The experience thus acquired is akin to that of the expert print-collector or the special-ized philatelist. The bibliographer's ideal would be to compel each and every volume to tell its own history; the clues by which this goal may in many cases be attained would not displease the mind of the modern reader of mystery-fiction, and the brain of an ideal bibliographer, tracing the pedigree of a manuscript, works not infrequently in the same grooves as the ideal detective of Sir Arthur Conan Doyle.

It may not be amiss to classify here the principal clues by which the history of a book may be ascertained, proceeding from the outside of the book to the inside, from the binding and cover to the contents, from the fly-leaves to the title-page and colophon-leaf.

First of all let us examine the binding: in most catalogues, a binding is merely described as 'old' or 'contemporary'. Now it only takes a little experience and observation to date a binding within much narrower limits. The date of an English binding may always be stated, allowing for very small chances of error, with an approximation of not more than thirty years. In a carefully worded description the words 'English red morocco binding, about 1700–1730' are already in themselves a valuable clue. Whenever a binding is signed or may be definitely ascribed to a given artist, the fact should be carefully noted, as individual collectors have always been apt to have their favourite binders. The Earl of Oxford, for instance, went to Elliot and Chapman, and Sir John Thorold, about 1830, was unwise enough to monopolize the services of that second-rate artist Richard Storr of Grantham.

Other collectors dictated to binders their preference for a particular style of binding: Ireland's 'green livery' was well known to the bibliophiles of 1810; Charles Lewis seldom used his vellum doublures, save in books bound for the Holford library. Lord Pembroke's dull red morocco is familiar to many lovers of early printed books.

It is obvious that armorial bearings, stamped on the covers, give an immediate clue to the early owner of a volume. A very useful help to the identification of such bearings is Cyril Davenport's *English Heraldic Bookstamps* (London, 1909, 4to), a collection which, however, is very far from complete. A few years ago, Messrs Ellis of New Bond Street had brought together and catalogued a large series of books in English armorial bindings, the description of which contains much new material supplementary to that gathered by Davenport.

Nor are marks of ownership confined to coats-of-arms. On

many volumes we find the owner's name stamped in full, e.g. Edward Gwynn, in the early seventeenth century; on many more, his initials, usually very difficult to identify. Crests and emblems, generally stamped on the back, have to be identified and memorized: the Fountaine elephant, the Pearson bird, the Essex initials SX, and many others to be mentioned hereafter.

The reverse of the upper cover and the opposite fly-leaf are the happiest hunting-grounds of the pedigree-chaser. It is there, when the modern binder and, worst of all, the modern bookseller, have not erased them—for pedigrees, however welcome to the scholar, have occasionally their drawbacks for trade purposes —that early owners have been scribbling for over two centuries their names, their historical and critical remarks, the date, place and price of purchase, the cost of mending and binding or rebinding, the shelf-mark in old or new libraries, the sale-number in an ancient or modern auction, anything and everything that may assist the bibliographer of today in his historical identifications.

All this should be preserved and deciphered: do not remove from the binding a dirty little label with a numeral pasted on the back or the side; but rather examine it and decide from its size and form (circular or diamond-shaped) whether it leads us to the Bindley or the Heber sale catalogues: learn to recognize at a glance the Sunderland and Ashburnham shelf-marks, the Britwell pencilled numbers and the blue-pencil numerals of the Barrois sale.

If we attempt to classify these inscriptions with a little more detail, we may, I think, divide them as follows:

A. Shelf-marks, which in older libraries usually consist of three numerals or letters indicating the case, shelf and number on shelf.

B. Accession-numbers, referring presumably to an accession catalogue, which might possibly in some instances still be extant. The Phillipps manuscripts and the Spencer volumes in the Rylands library are all marked with a numeral indicating the order of accession to the library.

C. Sale-numbers, either pasted-on labels or written on the book with the auctioneer's pencil.

D. Book-plates, a subject on which a considerable literature exists.

E. Signatures or initials of the owner, occasionally marked with a stamp or die (e.g. Richard Heber) or replaced by an armorial stamp (as in many Roxburghe books).

These signatures are not infrequently accompanied by remarks concerning the acquisition or collation of the books.

As regards the acquisition, a book-lover will usually state the source of purchase, the date, and often the price. For the latter he may use a cipher, usually obtained by the substitution of a letter for each of the nine numerals and a tenth for the zero, these ten letters forming a word which is the collector's mark or trade-word. A well-known London bookseller uses the word TWICKENHAM, T standing for 1, W for 2, and so on, M meaning zero, so that 320 will be written IWM. Whenever we meet with books in which such a cipher is used, the bibliographer's first task must be to identify the code-word, an achievement which with a little practice is seldom extremely difficult.

To the price of the book, the collector often adds the price of the agent's commission, usually 5 or 10 per cent if the book has been secured in an auction sale, and, if necessary, the price of the binding. It is to be regretted that so many collectors have omitted to make note of all these particulars. We cannot be too grateful for the diligence in that respect of such great bibliophiles as Michael Wodhull, Richard Heber and W. H. Miller, whose manuscript entries have preserved, for future generations, the individual history of many thousands of volumes.

For the last two centuries the collector's first care, on securing a volume, has been to collate it and to find out if it was complete. This enabled him to pencil on the fly-leaf the words 'collated and perfect', often abbreviated to 'c. & p.' and usually followed by the collector's initials or signature. It takes but a little visual memory to recognize at a glance the distinctive handwriting of such inscriptions, from the broad and powerful scrawl of Thomas Rawlinson, about 1720, to the minute pencilling of Cecil Dunn Gardner, 150 years later.

Other collectors were so strongly interested in their purchases that they scribbled on the fly-leaves remarks as to the contents and merits of each volume. Hanrott, for instance, pens careful bibliographical notes, while William Beckford's caustic comments are pencilled in a somewhat spiteful hand. Others, again, enter a reference to some standard bibliographical work, such as Panzer, in volumes from the Kloss library, or, in early English books, to the pages of Ames and Herbert.

In many cases the bookseller's prices are still inscribed at the beginning or end of the volume and the bibliographer soon learns to recognize the elder Pickering's clean figures or the collation marks of the firm of Quaritch.

Similar records occasionally adorn—or shall we say deface— the title-page; but usually they are confined to a signature or, as in the case of Narcissus Luttrell, to a purchase price.

Marks of ownership are seldom found in the body of the volume and instances like the Roxburghe stamp on the verso of the title or the initials of the owner, as in the Bliss books, added to the signatures of certain quires, remain sporadic.

Marginal notes and corrections, when clearly to be ascribed to a given author, may also assist in the tracing of a pedigree.

The literature of the subject is not a large one and only one satisfactory attempt has yet been made even to write a history of book-collecting in England.

Our knowledge of medieval English libraries owes much to the indefatigable labours of Montague Rhodes James and Sydney C. Cockerell.

W. Y. Fletcher's book on *English Book-Collectors* (London, 1902, 8vo) is extremely useful, but hardly technical enough for the student's purpose. For the biography of individual collectors, the *Dictionary of National Biography* is an inexhaustible mine of information, the lives of connoisseurs and scholars having received the particular attention of the editors.

Several attempts have been made in the last centuries to condense information respecting the manuscripts existing in British libraries. As early as 1600, an eminent bibliographer, Sir Thomas Bodley's friend, Thomas James, described the Oxford and Cambridge manuscripts in his *Ecloga Oxonio-Cantabrigiensis* (London, 1600, 4to).

A century later a more ambitious attempt was made by Edward Bernard in his *Catalogi librorum manuscriptorum* (1697), one of the most notable achievements of early English bibliographers.[1] In a stately folio volume, he contrived to print full catalogues of the manuscripts in all the Oxford libraries, shorter notices of those in Cambridge—where his plan seems to have been encouraged with hesitation—and lists, varying in quality, of manuscripts belonging to various cathedrals and schools and to over fifty private individuals; for many of the latter, Bernard's account is the only one in print and therefore of great value to scholars.

When G. Haenel, in 1830, printed his *Catalogi librorum manuscriptorum*, he thought so much of Bernard's work that he endeavoured to supplement him, rather than to duplicate his lists.[2]

Dibdin's *Bibliomania*,[3] *Bibliographical Decameron*,[4] and *Reminiscences*,[5] as also Clarke's *Reportorium bibliographicum*,[6] supply us with first-hand information on all the great collectors of the late eight-

[1] Edward Bernard, *Catalogi librorum manuscriptorum Angliae et Hiberniae in unum collecti cum indice alphabetico* (Oxford, University Press, 1697, Fol.). In 1850, Sir Thomas Phillipps printed an interesting table showing the changes of ownership of some of the libraries catalogued by Bernard (*Catalogus MSS. Magnae Britanniae*, i, pp. iii-iv).

[2] G. Haenel, *Catalogi librorum manuscriptorum qui in bibliothecis Galliae, Helvetiae, Belgii, Britanniae M., Hispaniae, Lusitaniae asservantur, nunc primum editi* (Leipzig, 1830, 4to). For the United Kingdom, see cols. 777–910.

[3] T. F. Dibdin, *Bibliomania*, new edition (London, 1842, 2 vols, 8vo). Reprinted in 1 vol. (London, 1876, 8vo).

[4] T. F. Dibdin, *The Bibliographical Decameron* (London, 1817, 3 vols, 8vo).

[5] T. F. Dibdin, *Reminiscences of a Literary Life* (London, 1836, 2 vols, 8vo).

[6] William Clarke, *Reportorium bibliographicum; or some account of the most celebrated British libraries* (London, 1819, 8vo).

eenth and early nineteenth centuries, supplemented, in a somewhat fragmentary manner, for the Victorian period by Bernard Quaritch's *Dictionary of English Book-Collectors.*[1]

W. C. Hazlitt's *Roll of Honour*[2] is a curious list of over 15,000 names, with hardly a fact inserted to make it really useful.

Many private collections of manuscripts are described in the invaluable series of *Reports of the Royal Commission on Historical Manuscripts* issued since 1870.

The catalogues of English book-sales, the earliest of which is that of Dr Lazarus Seaman (31 October 1676), form a most valuable source of information and one which has never been sufficiently made use of. The best series in existence is that belonging to the British Museum, of which a most useful catalogue has been compiled by Harold Mattingly and I. A. K. Burnett.[3] This great collection of over 8,000 English catalogues is especially valuable because it contains the auctioneers' own files of several important firms: Messrs Sotheby, from 1744, then started as S. Baker, to the present day, Messrs Evans (1812–45), Wheatley (1825–37), Lewis (1825–52), Southgate (1825–68), and Puttick and Simpson (from 1846).

The last years of Messrs Sotheby's and Puttick's catalogues are preserved at the auctioneers' offices, where students may consult them. Likewise, Messrs Christie (from 1760) and Hodgson (from 1807) have kept on their premises the whole files of their catalogues and have always been willing to allow them to be used for purposes of research. All the above-mentioned catalogues are fully annotated with prices and purchasers' names.

For catalogues not included in the above series, it is often very

[1] B. Quaritch, *Contributions towards a Dictionary of English Book-Collectors* (London, 1892–1921, 14 parts in 1 vol., 8vo).

[2] W. C. Hazlitt, *A Roll of Honour, a calendar of the names of over 17,000 men and women who throughout the British Isles and in our early Colonies have collected manuscripts and printed books* (London, 1908, 4to). Had first appeared in a much shorter form in Quaritch's *Dictionary of English Blook-Collectors*, part XII (1898).

[3] *List of Catalogues of English Book Sales, 1676–1900, now in the British Museum* (London, British Museum, 1915, 8vo).

difficult to locate a copy: outside the British Museum, there does not seem to exist a large collection of English catalogues. The Cambridge and Oxford libraries are somewhat disappointing in that respect and the only two good series in America, those in the New York Public Library and the Grolier Club, although fine, are far from complete; nevertheless, for American auctions, they are by far the best of their kind.

There is unfortunately no index to these thousands of catalogues and it is often a matter of long hours of tedious labour to trace in them the appearance or appearances of any given volume. To the best of my knowledge, this has only been attempted for two classes of books: for Shakespeare Quartos by Miss Bartlett and Mr Pollard,[1] and, for Caxton's impressions, by Blades and by myself.

Since 1887, however, *Book Prices Current* (or, since 1903, the parallel publication *Book Auction Records*) have given us full accounts of all the modern sales and *American Book Prices Current*, since 1895, fulfil the same office for American auctions.

From 1887 to 1913, *Book Prices Current* summarize each sale separately, with indexes for each year and three general indexes for decennial periods (1887–97, 1897–1906, 1907–16); since 1914, following the example of the American publication, the sales of each year are condensed into one alphabetical series, a system which combines with certain drawbacks several distinct advantages.

Manuscripts and autographs are included in *American Book Prices Current*, but not in the English series.[2]

May I add as a warning that, in spite of the care with which these volumes are edited, the serious student should always check them by referring to the actual catalogues of the sales?

Another source of information, hardly less valuable, would be

---

[1] H. C. Bartlett and A. W. Pollard, *A Census of Shakepeare's Plays in Quarto* (New Haven, Yale University Press, 1916, 4to).

[2] For English autograph sales, 1914–22, see *Autograph Prices Current*, I–VI (no more published).

the priced catalogues issued by booksellers throughout the eighteenth and nineteenth centuries, if only such catalogues were anywhere available for reference in really complete files. Unfortunately, none of the great British libraries seems to have preserved them systematically and the copyright laws seem to have omitted insuring their registration and filing. The British Museum collections are very inadequate in that respect and it is to be hoped that attempts will be made to remedy such a serious deficiency.

It would be highly interesting to locate the files of each bookseller's own copies of his catalogues, like the Payne and Foss series belonging to the Grolier Club.[1]

[1] I have just had brought to my notice the existence of a very interesting pamphlet by the late Hampton L. Carson, *Pedigrees in the Ownership of Law Books, an address delivered before the Philobiblon Club, January 28, 1915* (Philadelphia, 1916, 4to).

John Carter

5. *The format of books**

Format: this term (nowadays pronounced to rhyme with door-mat) is defined by *O.E.D.* as 'the shape and size of a book'. In bibliographical contexts it is used to indicate the size of a volume in terms of the number of times the original printed sheet has been folded to form its constituent leaves: modified when necessary by the subsequent make-up. Thus in a folio each sheet has been folded once, in a quarto twice, in an octavo three times; the size being thus respectively a half, a quarter and an eighth that of the original sheet. If the folded sheets have been gathered straightforwardly for sewing, then size and format will be indicated by a single term, e.g. quarto: if otherwise, the format of the completed volume will be expressed as, e.g. quarto in eights. The methods of folding in books of the smaller sizes (especially 12mo and 24mo) have often varied and the bibliographical results are sufficiently complicated to drive most amateurs to McKerrow (pp. 164 and following). But though the sizes of sheets vary substantially, thus producing subdivisions in the size of books, a terminology based on the method of folding has been found satisfactory for all but eccentrically shaped volumes.

The principal formats, with their common abbreviations, are:

* From *ABC for Book-Collectors* (London: Rupert Hart-Davis, 1952, revised 1967).

Folio (Fo., of late years sometimes $1°$).
Quarto (Qto, 4to, $4°$).
Octavo (Oct., 8vo, $8°$).
Duodecimo (12mo, $12°$, sometimes pronounced twelvemo).
Sextodecimo (16mo, usually pronounced sixteenmo).
Vicesimo-quarto (24mo, pronounced twentyfourmo).
Tricesimo-secundo (32mo, pronounced thirtytwomo).

The most considerable variation within these main sizes occurs, naturally, among folios and quartos, which are most nearly related to the source of variation: the sheet as produced by the papermaker. And it is the technical terms of the paper trade which provide the names—such as pott and elephant—for these sub-categories of size. But most booksellers' catalogues nowadays dispense with a terminology which is increasingly unfamiliar to, and unnecessarily technical for, the majority of their readers. These know—or should know—that a folio is a large upright-shaped volume and an octavo a small upright-shaped volume, while a quarto (between them in size) is essentially squarish in shape. And where special precision is necessary—to distinguish between different issues or variants, or to establish a large paper copy—this is commonly effected by giving the measurements of the leaf. (Incidentally, it will be a happy day for collectors when bibliographers and cataloguers settle unanimously either for inches or for centimetres as the accepted unit.)

Large folio, small folio, large quarto, small quarto are terms in constant use. But even the four main subdivisions of format, which may theoretically be applied to any size from 4to downwards, are in practice almost never used for anything but 4to and 8vo. As 8vo has been much the commonest format since very early days, approximate measurements of an 8vo page only are attached;

Foolscap 8vo	$6\frac{3}{4} \times 4\frac{1}{4}$ inches
Crown 8vo	$7\frac{1}{2} \times 5$ inches
Demy 8vo	$8\frac{3}{4} \times 5\frac{5}{8}$ inches
Royal 8vo	$10 \times 6\frac{1}{4}$ inches

Foolscap is sometimes abbreviated to f'cap. Demy is pronounced to rhyme with defy.

To understand format, read R. B. McKerrow, *An Introduction to Bibliography for Literary Students* (Oxford, 1927, corrected 1928): see also Graham Pollard's 'Notes on the Size of the Sheet' (*The Library*, Sept.–Dec. 1941).

6. *The rationale of copy-text**

When, in his edition of Nashe, McKerrow invented the term 'copy-text', he was merely giving a name to a conception already familiar, and he used it in a general sense to indicate that early text of a work which an editor selected as the basis of his own. Later, as we shall see, he gave it a somewhat different and more restricted meaning. It is this change in conception and its implications that I wish to consider.

The idea of treating some one text, usually of course a manuscript, as possessing over-riding authority originated among classical scholars, though something similar may no doubt be traced in the work of biblical critics. So long as purely eclectic methods prevailed, any preference for one manuscript over another, if it showed itself, was of course arbitrary; but when, towards the middle of last century, Lachmann and others introduced the genealogical classification of manuscripts as a principle of textual criticism, this appeared to provide at least some scientific basis for the conception of the most authoritative text. The genealogical method was the greatest advance ever made in this field, but its introduction was not unaccompanied by error. For lack of logical analysis, it led, at the hands of its less discriminating

* From *The Collected Papers of W. W. Greg*, edited by J. C. Maxwell (Oxford: Clarendon Press, 1966), pp. 374–91. The paper was read before the English Institute, New York on 8 September 1949 by Dr J. M. Osborn for W. W. Greg, and first published in *Studies in Bibliography* (Virginia) iii (1950–51), pp. 19–36.

exponents, to an attempt to reduce textual criticism to a code of mechanical rules. There was just this much excuse, that the method did make it possible to sweep away mechanically a great deal of rubbish. What its more hasty devotees failed to understand, or at any rate sufficiently to bear in mind, was that authority is never absolute, but only relative. Thus a school arose, mainly in Germany, that taught that if a manuscript could be shown to be generally more correct than any other and to have descended from the archetype independently of other lines of transmission, it was 'scientific' to follow its readings whenever they were not manifestly impossible. It was this fallacy that Housman exposed with devastating sarcasm. He had only to point out that 'Chance and the common course of nature will not bring it to pass that the readings of a MS are right wherever they are possible and impossible wherever they are wrong'[1]. That if a scribe makes a mistake he will inevitably produce nonsense is the tacit and wholly unwarranted assumption of the school in question,[2] and it is one that naturally commends itself to those who believe themselves capable of distinguishing between sense and nonsense, but who know themselves incapable of distinguishing between right and wrong. Unfortunately the attractions of a mechanical method misled many who were capable of better things.

There is one important respect in which the editing of classical texts differs from that of English. In the former it is the common practice, for fairly obvious reasons, to normalize the spelling, so that (apart from emendation) the function of an editor is limited to choosing between those manuscript readings that offer significant variants. In English it is now usual to preserve the spelling

[1] Introduction to Manilius, 1903, p. xxxii.

[2] The more naïve the scribe, the more often will the assumption prove correct; the more sophisticated, the less often. This, no doubt, is why critics of this school tend to reject 'the more correct but the less sincere' manuscript in favour of 'the more corrupt but the less interpolated', as Housman elsewhere observes ('The Application of Thought to Textual Criticism', *Proceedings of the Classical Association*, 1921, xviii. 75). Still, any reasonable critic will prefer the work of a naïve to to that of a sophisticated scribe, though he may not regard it as necessarily 'better'.

of the earliest or it may be some other selected text. Thus it will be seen that the conception of 'copy-text' does not present itself to the classical and to the English editor in quite the same way; indeed, if I am right in the view I am about to put forward, the classical theory of the 'best' or 'most authoritative' manuscript, whether it be held in a reasonable or in an obviously fallacious form, has really nothing to do with the English theory of 'copy-text' at all.

I do not wish to argue the case of 'old spelling' versus 'modern spelling'; I accept the view now prevalent among English scholars. But I cannot avoid some reference to the ground on which present practice is based, since it is intimately connected with my own views on copy-text. The former practice of modernizing the spelling of English works is no longer popular with editors, since spelling is now recognized as an essential characteristic of an author, or at least of his time and locality. So far as my knowledge goes, the alternative of normalization has not been seriously explored, but its philological difficulties are clearly considerable.[1] Whether, with the advance of linguistic science, it will some day be possible to establish a standard spelling for a particular period or district or author, or whether the historical circumstances in which our language has developed must always forbid any attempt of the sort (at any rate before comparatively recent times) I am not competent to say; but I agree with what appears to be the general opinion that such an attempt would at present only result in confusion and misrepresentation. It is therefore the modern editorial practice to choose whatever extant text may be supposed to represent most nearly what the author wrote and to follow it with the least possible alteration. But here we need to draw a distinction between the significant, or as I shall call them 'substantive', readings of the text, those namely that affect the

---

[1] I believe that an attempt has been made in the case of certain Old and Middle English texts, but how consistently and with what success I cannot judge. In any case I am here concerned chiefly with works of the sixteenth and seventeenth centuries.

author's meaning or the essence of his expression, and others, such in general as spelling, punctuation, word-division, and the like, affecting mainly its formal presentation, which may be regarded as the accidents, or as I shall call them 'accidentals', of the text.[1] The distinction is not arbitrary or theoretical, but has an immediate bearing on textual criticism, for scribes (or compositors) may in general be expected to react, and experience shows that they generally do react, differently to the two categories. As regards substantive readings their aim may be assumed to be to reproduce exactly those of their copy, though they will doubtless sometimes depart from them accidentally and may even, for one reason or another, do so intentionally: as regards accidentals they will normally follow their own habits or inclination, though they may, for various reasons and to varying degrees, be influenced by their copy. Thus a contemporary manuscript will at least preserve the spelling of the period, and may even retain some of the author's own, while it may at the same time depart frequently from the wording of the original; on the other hand a later transcript of the same original may reproduce the wording with essential accuracy while completely modernizing the spelling. Since, then, it is only on grounds of expediency, and in consequence either of philological ignorance or of linguistic circumstances, that we select a particular original as our copy-text, I suggest that it is only in the matter of accidentals that we are bound (within reason) to follow it, and that in respect of substantive readings we have exactly the same liberty (and obligation) of choice as has a classical editor, or as we should have were it a modernized text that we were preparing.[2]

[1] It will, no doubt, be objected that punctuation may very seriously 'affect' an author's meaning; still it remains properly a matter of presentation, as spelling does in spite of its use in distinguishing homonyms. The distinction I am trying to draw is practical, not philosophic. It is also true that between substantive readings and spellings there is an intermediate class of word-forms about the assignment of which opinions may differ and which may have to be treated differently in dealing with the work of different scribes.

[2] For the sake of clearness in making the distinction I have above stressed the independence of scribes and compositors in the matter of accidentals: at the same

But the distinction has not been generally recognized, and has never, so far as I am aware, been explicitly drawn.[1] This is not surprising. The battle between 'old spelling' and 'modern spelling' was fought out over works written for the most part between 1550 and 1650, and for which the original authorities are therefore as a rule printed editions. Now printed editions usually form an ancestral series, in which each is derived from its immediate predecessor; whereas the extant manuscripts of any work have usually only a collateral relationship, each being derived from the original independently, or more or less independently, of the others. Thus in the case of printed books, and in the absence of revision in a later edition, it is normally the first edition alone that can claim authority, and this authority naturally extends to substantive readings and accidentals alike. There was, therefore, little to force the distinction upon the notice of editors of works of the sixteenth and seventeenth centuries, and it apparently never occurred to them that some fundamental difference of editorial method might be called for in the rare cases in which a later edition had been revised by the author or in which there existed more than one 'substantive' edition of comparable authority.[2] Had they been more familiar with works transmitted

time, when he selects his copy-text, an editor will naturally hope that it retains at least something of the character of the original. Experience, however, shows that while the distribution of substantive variants generally agrees with the genetic relation of the texts, that of accidental variants is comparatively arbitrary.

[1] Some discussion bearing on it will be found in the Prolegomena to my lectures on *The Editorial Problem in Shakespeare* (1942), 'Note on Accidental Characteristics of the Text' (pp. l–lv), particularly the paragraph on pp. liii–liv, and note 1. But at the time of writing I was still a long way from any consistent theory regarding copy-text.

[2] A 'substantive' edition is McKerrow's term for an edition that is not a reprint of any other. I shall use the term in this sense, since I do not think that there should be any danger of confusion between 'substantive editions' and 'substantive readings'.

I have above ignored the practice of some eccentric editors who took as copy-text for a work the latest edition printed in the author's lifetime, on the assumption, presumably, that he revised each edition as it appeared. The textual results were naturally deplorable.

in manuscript, they might possibly have reconsidered their methods and been led to draw the distinction I am suggesting. For although the underlying principles of textual criticism are, of course, the same in the case of works transmitted in manuscripts and in print, particular circumstances differ, and certain aspects of the common principles may emerge more clearly in the one case than in the other. However, since the idea of copy-text originated and has generally been applied in connection with the editing of printed books, it is such that I shall mainly consider, and in what follows reference may be understood as confined to them unless manuscripts are specifically mentioned.

The distinction I am proposing between substantive readings and accidentals, or at any rate its relevance to the question of copy-text, was clearly not present to McKerrow's mind when in 1904 he published the second volume of his edition of the Works of Thomas Nashe, which included *The Unfortunate Traveller*. Collation of the early editions of this romance led him to the conclusion that the second, advertised on the title as 'Newly corrected and augmented', had in fact been revised by the author, but at the same time that not all the alterations could with certainty be ascribed to him.[1] He nevertheless proceeded to enunciate the rule that 'if an editor has reason to suppose that a certain text embodies later corrections than any other, and at the same time has no ground for disbelieving that these corrections, *or some of them at least*, are the work of the author, he has no choice but to make that text the basis of his reprint'.[2] The italics are mine.[3]

---

[1] He believed, or at least strongly suspected, that some were due to the printer's desire to save space, and that others were 'the work of some person who had not thoroughly considered the sense of the passage which he was altering' (ii. 195).

[2] Nashe, ii. 197. The word 'reprint' really begs the question. If all an 'editor' aims at is an exact reprint, then obviously he will choose one early edition, on whatever grounds he considers relevant, and reproduce it as it stands. But McKerrow does emend his copy-text where necessary. It is symptomatic that he did not distinguish between a critical edition and a reprint.

[3] Without the italicized phrase the statement would appear much more plausible (though I should still regard it as fallacious, and so would McKerrow himself have done later on) but it would not justify the procedure adopted.

This is applying with a vengeance the principle that I once approvingly described as 'maintaining the integrity of the copy-text'. But it must be pointed out that there are in fact two quite distinct principles involved. One, put in more general form, is that if, for whatever reason, a particular authority be on the whole preferred, an editor is bound to accept all its substantive readings (if not manifestly impossible). This is the old fallacy of the 'best text', and may be taken to be now generally rejected. The other principle, also put in general form, is that whatever particular authority be preferred, whether as being revised or as generally preserving the substantive readings more faithfully than any other, it must be taken as copy-text, that is to say that it must also be followed in the matter of accidentals. This is the principle that interests us at the moment, and it is one that McKerrow himself came, at least partly, to question.

In 1939 McKerrow published his *Prolegomena for the Oxford Shakespeare*, and he would not have been the critic he was if his views had not undergone some changes in the course of thirty-five years. One was in respect of revision. He had come to the opinion that to take a reprint, even a revised reprint, as copy-text was indefensible. Whatever may be the relation of a particular substantive edition to the author's manuscript (provided that there is any transcriptional link at all) it stands to reason that the relation of a reprint of that edition must be more remote. If then, putting aside all question of revision, a particular substantive edition has an over-riding claim to be taken as copy-text, to displace it in favour of a reprint, whether revised or not, means receding at least one step further from the author's original in so far as the general form of the text is concerned.[1] Some such considerations must have been in McKerrow's mind when he wrote (*Prolegomena*, pp. 17–18): 'Even if, however, we were to assure ourselves . . . that certain corrections found in a later edition of a play were of Shakespearian authority, it would not by any

[1] This may, at any rate, be put forward as a general proposition, leaving possible exceptions to be considered later (pp. 154 ff.).

means follow that that edition should be used as the copy-text of a reprint.[1] It would undoubtedly be necessary to incorporate these corrections in our text, but . . . it seems evident that . . . this later edition will (except for the corrections) deviate more widely than the earliest print from the author's original manuscript. . . . [Thus] the nearest approach to our ideal . . . will be produced by using the earliest "good" print as copy-text and inserting into it, from the first edition which contains them, such corrections as appear to us to be derived from the author.' This is a clear statement of the position, and in it he draws exactly the distinction between substantive readings (in the form of corrections) and accidentals (or general texture) on which I am insisting. He then, however, relapsed into heresy in the matter of the substantive readings. Having spoken, as above, of the need to introduce 'such corrections as appear to us to be derived from the author', he seems to have feared conceding too much to eclecticism, and he proceeded: 'We are not to regard the "goodness" of a reading in and by itself, or to consider whether it appeals to our aesthetic sensibilities or not; we are to consider whether a particular edition taken *as a whole* contains variants from the edition from which it was otherwise printed which could not reasonably be attributed to an ordinary press-corrector, but by reason of their style, point, and what we call inner harmony with the spirit of the play as a whole, seem likely to be the work of the author: and once having decided this to our satisfaction we must accept *all* the alterations of that edition, saving any which seem obvious blunders or misprints.' We can clearly see enough what he had in mind, namely that the evidence of correction (under which head he presumably intended to include revision) must be considered *as a whole*; but he failed to add the equally important proviso that the alterations must also be *of a piece* (and not, as in *The Unfortunate Traveller*, of apparently disparate origin) before we can be called upon to accept them *all*. As he states it his canon is open to exactly the same

[1] Again he speaks of a 'reprint' where he evidently had in mind a critical edition on conservative lines.

objections as the 'most authoritative manuscript' theory in classical editing.

McKerrow was, therefore, in his later work quite conscious of the distinction between substantive readings and accidentals, in so far as the problem of revision is concerned. But he never applied the conception to cases in which we have more than one substantive text, as in *Hamlet* and perhaps in *2 Henry IV*, *Troilus and Cressida*, and *Othello*. Presumably he would have argued that since faithfulness to the wording of the author was one of the criteria he laid down for determining the choice of the copy-text, it was an editor's duty to follow its substantive readings with a minimum of interference.

We may assume that neither McKerrow nor other editors of the conservative school imagined that such a procedure would always result in establishing the authentic text of the original; what they believed was that from it less harm would result than from opening the door to individual choice among variants, since it substituted an objective for a subjective method of determination. This is, I think, open to question. It is impossible to exclude individual judgement from editorial procedure: it operates of necessity in the all-important matter of the choice of copy-text and in the minor one of deciding what readings are possible and what are not; why, therefore, should the choice between possible readings be withdrawn from its competence? Uniformity of result at the hands of different editors is worth little if it means only uniformity in error; and it may not be too optimistic a belief that the judgement of an editor, fallible as it must necessarily be, is likely to bring us closer to what the author wrote than the enforcement of an arbitrary rule.

The true theory is, I contend, that the copy-text should govern (generally) in the matter of accidentals, but that the choice between substantive readings belongs to the general theory of textual criticism and lies altogether beyond the narrow principle of the copy-text. Thus it may happen that in a critical edition the text rightly chosen as copy may not by any means be the one that supplies most substantive readings in cases of variation. The failure to make this distinction and to apply this principle has naturally led to too close and too general a reliance upon the text chosen as basis for an edition, and there has arisen what may be called the tyranny of the copy-text,[1] a tyranny that has, in my opinion, vitiated much of the best editorial work of the past generation.

I will give a couple of examples of the sort of thing I mean that I have lately come across in the course of my own work. They are all the more suitable as illustrations since they occur in texts edited by scholars of recognized authority, neither of whom is particularly subject to the tyranny in question. One is from the edition of Marlowe's *Doctor Faustus* by Professor F. S. Boas (1932). The editor, rightly I think, took the so-called B-text (1616) as the basis of his own, correcting it where necessary by comparison with the A-text (1604).[2] Now a famous line in Faustus's opening soliloquy runs in 1604,

> Bid *Oncaymæon* farewell, *Galen* come

and in 1616,

> Bid *Oeconomy* farewell; and *Galen* come . . .

Here '*Oncaymæon*' is now recognized as standing for '*on cay mæ on*' or ὄν καὶ μὴ ὄν: but this was not understood at the time, and '*Oeconomy*' was substituted in reprints of the A-text in 1609 and 1611, and thence taken over by the B-text. The change, however, produced a rather awkward line, and in 1616 the 'and' was introduced as a metrical accommodation. In the first half of the line Boas rightly restored the reading implied in A; but in the second half he retained, out of deference to his copy-text, the

---

[1] [I think the phrase 'the tyranny of the copy-text' was first used by Paul Maas in connection with the Prolegomena in my book *The Editorial Problem in Shakespeare*. But what he then had in mind was the decision to preserve 'old spelling'. (See *The Review of English Studies*, April 1944. xx. 159.)]

[2] Boas's text is in fact modernized, so that my theory of copy-text does not strictly apply, but since he definitely accepts the B-text as his authority, the principle is the same.

'and' whose only object was to accommodate the reading he had rejected in the first. One could hardly find a better example of the contradictions to which a mechanical following of the copy-text may lead.[1]

My other instance is from *The Gipsies Metamorphosed* as edited by Dr Percy Simpson among the masques of Ben Jonson in 1941. He took as his copy-text the Huntington manuscript, and I entirely agree with his choice. In this, and in Simpson's edition, a line of the ribald Cock Lorel ballad runs (sir-reverence!),

All wch he blewe away with a fart

whereas for *blewe* other authorities have *flirted*. Now, the meaning of *flirted* is not immediately apparent, for no appropriate sense of the word is recorded. There is, however, a rare use of the substantive *flirt* for a sudden gust of wind, and it is impossible to doubt that this is what Jonson had in mind, for no scribe or compositor could have invented the reading *flirted*. It follows that in the manuscript *blewe* is nothing but the conjecture of a scribe who did not understand his original: only the mesmeric influence of the copy-text could obscure so obvious a fact.[2]

I give these examples merely to illustrate the kind of error that, in modern editions of English works, often results from undue deference to the copy-text. This reliance on one particular authority results from the desire for an objective theory of text-construction and a distrust, often no doubt justified, of the operation of individual judgement. The attitude may be explained

[1] Or consider the following readings: 1604, 1609 'Consissylogismes', 1611 'subtile sylogismes', 1616 'subtle Sillogismes'. Here 'subtile', an irresponsible guess by the printer of 1611 for a word he did not understand, was taken over in 1616. The correct reading is, of course, 'concise syllogisms'. Boas's refusal to take account of the copy used in 1616 led him here and elsewhere to perpetuate some of its manifest errors. In this particular instance he appears to have been unaware of the reading of 1611.

[2] At another point two lines appear in an unnatural order in the manuscript. The genetic relation of the texts proves the inversion to be an error. But of this relation Simpson seems to have been ignorant. He was again content to rely on the copy-text.

historically as a natural and largely salutary reaction against the methods of earlier editors. Dissatisfied with the results of eclectic freedom and reliance on personal taste, critics sought to establish some sort of mechanical apparatus for dealing with textual problems that should lead to uniform results independent of the operator. Their efforts were not altogether unattended by success. One result was the recognition of the general worthlessness of reprints. And even in the more difficult field of manuscript transmission it is true that formal rules will carry us part of the way: they can at least effect a preliminary clearing of the ground. This I sought to show in my essay on *The Calculus of Variants* (1927); but in the course of investigation it became clear that there is a definite limit to the field over which formal rules are applicable. Between readings of equal extrinsic authority no rules of the sort can decide, since by their very nature it is only to extrinsic relations that they are relevant. The choice is necessarily a matter for editorial judgement, and an editor who declines or is unable to exercise his judgement and falls back on some arbitrary canon, such as the authority of the copy-text, is in fact abdicating his editorial function. Yet this is what has been frequently commended as 'scientific'—'streng wissenschaftlich' in the prevalent idiom—and the result is that what many editors have done is to produce, not editions of their authors' works at all, but only editions of particular authorities for those works, a course that may be perfectly legitimate in itself, but was not the one they were professedly pursuing.

This by way, more or less, of digression. At the risk of repetition I should like to recapitulate my view of the position of copy-text in editorial procedure. The thesis I am arguing is that the historical circumstances of the English language make it necessary to adopt in formal matters the guidance of some particular early text. If the several extant texts of a work form an ancestral series, the earliest will naturally be selected, and since this will not only come nearest to the author's original in accidentals, but also (revision apart) most faithfully preserve the correct readings where substantive variants are in question, everything is straightforward, and the conservative treatment of the copy-text is justified. But whenever there is more than one substantive text of comparable authority,[1] then although it will still be necessary to choose one of them as copy-text, and to follow it in accidentals, this copy-text can be allowed no over-riding or even preponderant authority so far as substantive readings are concerned. The choice between these, in cases of variation, will be determined partly by the opinion the editor may form respecting the nature of the copy from which each substantive edition was printed, which is a matter of external authority; partly by the intrinsic authority of the several texts as judged by the relative frequency of manifest errors therein; and partly by the editor's judgement of the in-trinsic claims of individual readings to originality—in other words their intrinsic merit, so long as by 'merit' we mean the likelihood of their being what the author wrote rather than their appeal to the individual taste of the editor.

Such, as I see it, is the general theory of copy-text. But there remain a number of subsidiary questions that it may be worth-while to discuss. One is the degree of faithfulness with which the copy-text should be reproduced. Since the adoption of a copy-text is a matter of convenience rather than of principle—being imposed on us either by linguistic circumstances or our own philological ignorance—it follows that there is no reason for treating it as sacrosanct, even apart from the question of substantive variation. Every editor aiming at a critical edition will, of course, correct scribal or typographical errors. He will also correct readings in accordance with any errata included in the edition taken as copy-text. I see no reason why he should not alter mis-leading or eccentric spellings which he is satisfied emanate from the scribe or compositor and not from the author. If the punctua-tion is persistently erroneous or defective an editor may prefer to

[1] The proviso is inserted to meet the case of the so-called 'bad quartos' of Shakespearian and other Elizabethan plays and of the whole class of 'reported' texts, whose testimony can in general be neglected.

discard it altogether to make way for one of his own. He is, I think, at liberty to do so, provided that he gives due weight to the original in deciding on his own, and that he records the alteration whenever the sense is appreciably affected. Much the same applies to the use of capitals and italics. I should favour expanding contractions (except perhaps when dealing with an author's holograph) so long as ambiguities and abnormalities are recorded. A critical edition does not seem to me a suitable place in which to record the graphic peculiarities of particular texts,[1] and in this respect the copy-text is only one among others. These, however, are all matters within the discretion of an editor: I am only concerned to uphold his liberty of judgement.

Some minor points arise when it becomes necessary to replace a reading of the copy-text by one derived from another source. It need not, I think, be copied in the exact form in which it there appears. Suppose that the copy-text follows the earlier convention in the use of u and v, and the source from which the reading is taken follows the later. Naturally in transferring the reading from the latter to the former it would be made to conform to the earlier convention. I would go further. Suppose that the copy-text reads 'hazard', but that we have reason to believe that the correct reading is 'venture': suppose further that whenever this word occurs in the copy-text it is in the form 'venter': then 'venter', I maintain, is the form we should adopt. In like manner editorial emendations should be made to conform to the habitual spelling of the copy-text.

In the case of rival substantive editions the choice between substantive variants is, I have explained, generally independent of the copy-text. Perhaps one concession should be made. Suppose that the claims of two readings, one in the copy-text and one in some other authority, appear to be exactly balanced: what then should an editor do? In such a case, while there can be no logical reason for giving preference to the copy-text, in practice, if there

[1] That is, certainly not in the text, and probably not in the general apparatus: they may appropriately form the subject of an appendix.

is no reason for altering its reading, the obvious thing seems to be to let it stand.[1]

Much more important, and difficult, are the problems that arise in connection with revision. McKerrow seems only to mention correction, but I think he must have intended to include revision, so long as this falls short of complete rewriting: in any case the principle is the same. I have already considered the practice he advocated (pp. 143–46)—namely that an editor should take the original edition as his copy-text and introduce into it all the substantive variants of the revised reprint, other than manifest errors—and have explained that I regard it as too sweeping and mechanical. The emendation that I proposed (pp. 146–47) is, I think, theoretically sufficient, but from a practical point of view it lacks precision. In a case of revision or correction the normal procedure would be for the author to send the printer either a list of the alterations to be made or else a corrected copy of an earlier edition. In setting up the new edition we may suppose that the printer would incorporate the alterations thus indicated by the author; but it must be assumed that he would also introduce a normal amount of unauthorized variation of his own.[2] The problem that faces the editor is to distinguish between the two categories. I suggest the following frankly subjective procedure.

[1] This is the course I recommended in the Prolegomena to *The Editorial Problem in Shakespeare* (p. xxix), adding that it 'at least saves the trouble of tossing a coin'. What I actually wrote in 1942 was that in such circumstances an editor 'will naturally retain the reading of the copy-text, this being the text which he has already decided is *prima facie* the more correct'. This implies that correctness in respect of substantive readings is one of the criteria in the choice of the copy-text; and indeed I followed McKerrow in laying it down that an editor should select as copy-text the one that 'appears likely to have departed least in wording, spelling, and punctuation from the author's manuscript'. There is a good deal in my Prolegomena that I should now express differently, and on this particular point I have definitely changed my opinion. I should now say that the choice of the copy-text depends solely on its formal features (accidentals) and that fidelity as regards substantive readings is irrelevant—though fortunately in nine cases out of ten the choice will be the same whichever rule we adopt.

[2] I mean substantive variation, such as occurs in all but the most faithful reprints.

Granting that the fact of revision (or correction) is established, an editor should in every case of variation ask himself (1) whether the original reading is one that can reasonably be attributed to the author, and (2) whether the later reading is one that the author can reasonably be supposed to have substituted for the former. If the answer to the first question is negative, then the later reading should be accepted as at least possibly an authoritative correction (unless of course, it is itself incredible). If the answer to (1) is affirmative and the answer to (2) is negative, the original reading should be retained. If the answers to both questions are affirmative, then the later reading should be presumed to be due to revision and admitted into the text, whether the editor himself considers it an improvement or not. It will be observed that one implication of this procedure is that a later variant that is either completely indifferent or manifestly inferior, or for the substitution of which no motive can be suggested, should be treated as fortuitous and refused admission to the text—to the scandal of faithful followers of McKerrow. I do not, of course, pretend that my procedure will lead to consistently correct results, but I think that the results, if less uniform, will be on the whole preferable to those achieved through following any mechanical rule. I am, no doubt, presupposing an editor of reasonable competence; but if an editor is really incompetent, I doubt whether it much matters what procedure he adopts: he may indeed do less harm with some than with others, he will do little good with any. And in any case, I consider that it would be disastrous to curb the liberty of competent editors in the hope of preventing fools from behaving after their kind.

I will give one illustration of the procedure in operation, taken again from Jonson's *Masque of Gipsies*, a work that is known to have been extensively revised for a later performance. At one point the text of the original version runs as follows:

a wise Gypsie . . . is as politicke a piece of Flesh, as most Iustices in the County where he maunds whereas the texts of the revised version replace *maunds* by *stalkes*. Now, *maund* is a recognized canting term meaning to beg, and there is not the least doubt that it is what Jonson originally wrote. Further, it might well be argued that it is less likely that he should have displaced it in revision by a comparatively commonplace alternative, than that a scribe should have altered a rather unusual word that he failed to understand—just as we know that, in a line already quoted (p. 148), a scribe altered *flirted* to *blewe*. I should myself incline to this view were it not that at another point Jonson in revision added the lines,

> And then ye may stalke
> The *Gypsies* walke

where *stalk*, in the sense of going stealthily, is used almost as a technical term. In view of this I do not think it unreasonable to suppose that Jonson himself substituted *stalkes* for *maunds* from a desire to avoid the implication that his aristocratic Gipsies were beggars, and I conclude that it must be allowed to pass as (at least possibly) a correction, though no reasonable critic would *prefer* it to the original.

With McKerrow's view that in all normal cases of correction or revision the original edition should still be taken as the copy-text, I am in complete agreement. But not all cases are normal, as McKerrow himself recognized. While advocating, in the passage already quoted (p. 145), that the earliest 'good' edition should be taken as copy-text and corrections incorporated in it, he added the proviso, 'unless we could show that the [revised] edition in question (or the copy from which it had been printed) had been gone over and corrected *throughout* by' the author (my italics). This proviso is not in fact very explicit, but it clearly assumes that there are (or at least may be) cases in which an editor would be justified in taking a revised reprint as his copy-text, and it may be worth inquiring what these supposed cases are. If a work has been entirely rewritten, and is printed from a new manuscript, the

question does not arise, since the revised edition will be a substantive one, and as such will presumably be chosen by the editor
as his copy-text. But short of this, an author, wishing to make
corrections or alterations in his work, may not merely hand the
printer a revised copy of an earlier edition, but himself supervise
the printing of the new edition and correct the proofs as the sheets
go through the press. In such a case it may be argued that even
though the earlier edition, if printed from his own manuscript,
will preserve the author's individual peculiarities more faithfully
than the revised reprint, he must nevertheless be assumed to have
taken responsibility for the latter in respect of accidentals no less
than substantive readings, and that it is therefore the revised
reprint that should be taken as copy-text.

The classical example is afforded by the plays in the 1616 folio
of Ben Jonson's Works. In this it appears that even the largely
recast *Every Man in his Humour* was not set up from an independent manuscript but from a much corrected copy of the quarto
of 1601. That Jonson revised the proofs of the folio has indeed
been disputed, but Simpson is most likely correct in supposing
that he did so, and he was almost certainly responsible for the
numerous corrections made while the sheets were in process of
printing. Simpson's consequent decision to take the folio for his
copy-text for the plays it contains will doubtless be approved
by most critics. I at least have no wish to dispute his choice.[1]
Only I would point out—and here I think Dr Simpson would
agree with me—that even in this case the procedure involves
some sacrifice of individuality. For example, I notice that in the
text of *Sejanus* as printed by him there are twenty-eight instances
of the Jonsonian 'Apostrophus' (an apostrophe indicating the elision
of a vowel that is nevertheless retained in printing) but of these
only half actually appear in the folio, the rest he has introduced
from the quarto. This amounts to an admission that in some

[1] Simpson's procedure in taking the 1616 folio as copy-text in the case of most
of the masques included, although he admits that in their case Jonson cannot
be supposed to have supervised the printing, is much more questionable.

respects at least the quarto preserves the formal aspect of the author's original more faithfully than the folio.

The fact is that cases of revision differ so greatly in circumstances and character that it seems impossible to lay down any hard and fast rule as to when an editor should take the original edition as his copy-text and when the revised reprint. All that can be said is that if the original be selected, then the author's corrections must be incorporated; and that if the reprint be selected, then the original reading must be restored when that of the reprint is due to unauthorized variation. Thus the editor cannot escape the responsibility of distinguishing to the best of his ability between the two categories. No juggling with copy-text will relieve him of the duty and necessity of exercising his own judgement.

In conclusion I should like to examine this problem of revision and copy-text a little closer. In the case of a work like *Sejanus*, in which correction or revision has been slight, it would obviously be possible to take the quarto as the copy-text and introduce into it whatever authoritative alterations the folio may supply; and indeed, were one editing the play independently, this would be the natural course to pursue. But a text like that of *Every Man in his Humour* presents an entirely different problem. In the folio, revision and reproduction are so blended that it would seem impossible to disentangle intentional from what may be fortuitous variation, and injudicious to make the attempt. An editor of the revised version has no choice but to take the folio as his copy-text. It would appear, therefore, that a reprint may in practice be forced upon an editor as copy-text by the nature of the revision itself, quite apart from the question whether or not the author exercised any supervision over its printing.

This has a bearing upon another class of texts, in which a reprint was revised, not by the author, but through comparison with some more authoritative manuscript. Instances are Shakespeare's *Richard III* and *King Lear*. Of both much the best text is supplied by the folio of 1623; but this is not a substantive text, but one set up from a copy of an earlier quarto that had been extensively corrected by collation with a manuscript preserved in the playhouse. So great and so detailed appears to have been the revision that it would be an almost impossible task to distinguish between variation due to the corrector and that due to the compositor,[1] and an editor has no choice but to take the folio as copy-text. Indeed, this would in any case be incumbent upon him for a different reason; for the folio texts are in some parts connected by transcriptional continuity with the author's manuscript, whereas the quartos contain, it is generally assumed, only reported texts, whose accidental characteristics can be of no authority whatever. At the same time, analogy with *Every Man in his Humour* suggests that even had the quartos of *Richard III* and *King Lear* possessed higher authority than in fact they do, the choice of copy-text must yet have been the same.

I began this discussion in the hope of clearing my own mind as well as others' on a rather obscure though not unimportant matter of editorial practice. I have done something to sort out my own ideas: others must judge for themselves. If they disagree, it is up to them to maintain some different point of view. My desire is rather to provoke discussion than to lay down the law.

---

[1] Some variation is certainly due to error on the part of the folio printer, and this it is of course the business of an editor to detect and correct so far as he is able.

R B McKerrow

7. *Form and matter in the publication of research**

May I, as one who has had occasion both as a publisher and an editor to read a very considerable number of books and articles embodying the results of research into English literary history, plead for more attention to *form* in the presentation of such work?

I do not know whether advancing age has made me thicker in the head than I used to be or whether I have merely become more impatient—there is so much that one still wants to do and constantly less and less time in which to do it—but it certainly seems to me that there has been a tendency in recent years for the way in which the results of research are set out to become progressively less efficient, especially among the younger students, both in England and in America. And when I say 'less efficient' I am not thinking of any high qualities of literary art, but of the simplest qualities of precision and intelligibility. Indeed, I have sometimes wondered whether the fate of 'English studies' will not eventually be to be smothered in a kind of woolly and impenetrable fog of wordiness that few or none will be bothered to penetrate.

It may perhaps surprise some readers of *R.E.S.* if I tell them that I have several times been compelled to refuse articles offered to me which seemed, from the evidence of the footnotes, to have been the product of real research, for no other reason than that after

* From *Review of English Studies* xvi (1940) (Oxford: Clarendon Press), pp. 116–21.

several readings I have completely failed to discover the point or points which the author was trying to make. In one or two cases this has perhaps been due to the author's inability to express himself in English at all, but in others the trouble has seemed to be rather due to a complete ignorance of the way in which he should present his material. Being himself fully cognizant of the point at issue and with the way in which his research corrects or supplements views currently held on his subject, the author has apparently assumed that all would become clear to his readers by the mere recital of his investigations without any commentary on the results as they appear to him. But such a mere recital of an investigation will only convey what is intended by the author to a person with the same knowledge and mental outlook as the author himself, and to anyone else may be almost meaningless.

Articles of which I have been unable to make out the point at all I have necessarily rejected, generally after trying them on a friend or two, lest I were at the time more than usually dense; but I must confess to having printed in R.E.S. a certain number of articles which I regarded as definitely bad work. These were some which contained good research which I was assured would be useful to those with knowledge of the subject and willing to spend time and effort in puzzling out the bearing of the new matter, but of little if any use to others. Such articles cannot, of course, be lightly rejected. The pity is they could so easily, by a writer of adequate training in presenting his facts, or with sufficient imagination to enable him to dispense with such training, have been made really interesting contributions to knowledge which would have appealed to a wide circle of readers, instead of only being absorbed with difficulty and distaste by the few.

For it is imagination which is, before all else, necessary in presenting a piece of research. It is not to be considered as, so to say, an emanation of the author's brain which has been allowed to escape into the void, a mere fragment of knowledge detached from its originator, but one which is intended to become part of the knowledge of others, and in order that it may do this it must be so shaped and adapted that it may fit with ease and certainty on to the knowledge of others, those others being, of course, the likely readers.

New facts, skilfully prepared for our easy assimilation, for forming part of our existing aggregate of knowledge, are invariably welcomed, even when the subject is not one in which we are normally much interested, when a badly presented bit of what should be our own special subject may completely fail to make any impression on our consciousness.

We ought, I think, at the start to realize that no readers whom we are likely to have will be nearly as much interested in our views or discoveries as we ourselves are. Most of them will be people who are a little tired, a little bored, and who read us rather out of a sense of duty and a wish to keep up with what is being done than because they have any real interest in the subject; and in return for our reader's complaisance it is our duty as well as our interest to put what we have to say before him with as little trouble to him as possible. It is our duty because we ought to be kind to our fellow creature; it is our interest because if the view that we wish to put before him is clearly and competently expressed, so that he understands without trouble what we are trying to say, he will be gratified at the smooth working of his own intelligence and will inevitably think better of our theory and of its author than if he had had to puzzle himself over what we mean and then in the end doubt whether he had really understood us, so raising in himself an uneasy doubt whether his brains are quite what they used to be!

Now I suggest that if we analyse almost any piece of research which seems to us thoroughly workmanlike and satisfactory from all points of view, we shall almost always find that it falls into five parts in the following order.

1. The *introduction*, in which the author briefly states the present position of research on his subject and the views currently held on it.

2. The *proposal*, in which he describes in outline what he hopes to prove.
3. The *boost*, in which he proceeds to magnify the importance of his discovery or argument and to explain what a revolution it will create in the views generally held on the whole period with which he is dealing. This is, as it were, a taste of sauce to stimulate the reader's appetite.
4. The *demonstration*, in which he sets forth his discovery or argument in an orderly fashion.
5. The *conclusion*, or *crow*, in which he summarizes what he claims to have shown, and points out how complete and unshakeable is his proof.

Of course I am not serious in this! It is not to be supposed necessary that we should *formally* divide our research articles in this way, but it is a real and practical division and there are few research articles which would not be improved by the adoption of such a framework, at least under the surface.

The following points might, I believe, be worth much more serious consideration than seems frequently to be given to them.
1. The subject of a research article should always be a unity. The paper should always deal either with a single subject or with a well-defined group of subjects of the same general character. Thus a particular literary work might be dealt with in all its aspects, or any one aspect might be dealt with, say, its origin, its date, its popularity, or what not, or its author's life or any one period or incident of it. On the other hand it is seldom well to mix two pieces of research on different scales, an account of a man's works as a whole and of a particular one of his works dealt with in much greater detail. Similarly, an article in which an attempt is made both to give new discoveries in an author's biography and a correction in the bibliography of one of his books will almost certainly turn out an unreadable muddle. These various kinds of discovery may often arise as the result of a single piece of research, but it is much better to put them

forward in quite independent articles. Opportunity may always be found to insert a cross-reference from one to the other in order to ensure that students do not overlook the author's other discoveries.

✓ 2. Give your book or article a name which tells at once what it is all about. Facetious and cryptic titles should be utterly eschewed. At best they annoy, and at worst they tend to be forgotten and to render the work under which they are concealed untraceable. Fancy names, pastoral and the like, should never be used, however familiar they may be to students versed in the literature of a particular period. Thus Katherine Philips may have been well known to students of her time as the 'Matchless Orinda', but one who writes about her by the latter name risks his work being entered in indexes under headings where it will be missed by scholars searching for her under her family name.

✓ 3. Remember that though the great majority of your readers are likely to have a considerable knowledge of English Literature as a whole and an expert knowledge of a certain part of it, only a minority are likely to be experts in your particular period or field. In any case very few indeed can be expected to possess the minute knowledge of it which you who have just been devoting all your time to the study of it have or ought to have. (Indeed, if you do not know *much* more than others, why are you writing about it?) Keep this in mind in the whole of your writing and *adjust what you say to the knowledge which you may reasonably expect your readers to have*. This is really the whole secret of exposition, and it is so simple that it seems incredible that writers of research articles should so often be ignorant of it. But they are, they are! If you have a young brother or sister of, say, fifteen years old or so, think that you have him or her before you and that you are trying to explain the point of your article to them and at the same time to prevent them from thinking what an ass you are to be wasting their time and yours about anything so completely futile. If in your imagination you see their eyes light up and their faces set with a desire to protest or argue, you will know that whether the thesis of your paper is sound or not its presentation is at least on the right lines!

Naturally the method of presenting an argument must depend on the persons for whom it is intended. You need not in an article in *R.E.S.* explain who Ben Jonson or John Dryden or Cynewulf or Laȝamon were, but it would be unwise to expect all your readers to have precise knowledge as to their dates or the details of their biography. If these are required for your argument it is easy to give them without the reader being moved to indignation by the feeling that he is being treated like a child. In this connection much offence may often be avoided by the insertion of the little phrases 'of course', or 'as everyone knows'—e.g. 'Stephen Hawes, who was of course writing in the earliest years of the sixteenth century, and called Lydgate "master" ' gives information which every reader of *R.E.S.* must have known at some time, but of which a few may need to be reminded in an article concerning the poetical associations of Henry VIII's court.

In your introduction, then, take your reader metaphorically by the hand and lead him gently up to the threshold of your research, reminding him courteously and without any appearance of dogmatism, not with the gestures of a teacher but gently as a comrade in study, of what he ought to know in order to understand what you have to tell him—the object of your research. He will be far better able to appreciate your demonstration if he knows what to look for, and to know what to look for if you tell him at once just what the current views of the matter are and how your own differ from them.

4. So far as possible state your facts in chronological order. When a digression is necessary, make quite clear that it *is* a digression, and when you reach the end of it, make quite clear that you are returning to the main course of the story. And always give plenty of dates, *real* dates, not the kind of dates of which many of the historical people seem to be so fond—'about two years before the conclusion of the events which we have described' or 'later in the same year', which after reading several earlier pages turns out

to be the year in which 'the king' attained his majority, necessitating further research to discover what king and in what year and what part of the year he was born and what 'majority' meant at the time. But enough! We have all suffered. Keep on remembering that though *you* are perhaps completely familiar with all aspects of your subject, your reader may not be.

5. State your facts as simply as possible, even boldly. No one wants flowers of eloquence or literary ornaments in a research article. On the other hand do not be slangy, and, especially if you are writing for *R.E.S.*, do not use American slang. We may be interested in it, but we may not always understand it. Only a few days ago I had to beg the author of an excellent article which I was printing to substitute some phrase more intelligible to us over in England for a statement that certain evidence—'is not quite enough to convict of actual skulduggery (and the aroma of high-binding will not down) . . .'

6. Never be cryptic nor use literary paraphrases. Needless mysteries are out of place in research articles. There are plenty of them there already. If they think that you are trying to be superior, most readers will stop reading at once.

7. Do not try to be humorous. Humour is well enough in its place, but nothing more infuriates a man who is looking for a plain statement of facts than untimely humour, especially if he does not know whether the writer is really trying to be humorous or not, a point which some would-be humorists fail to make clear.

8. Do not use ambiguous expressions. The worst of these are perhaps phrases containing the word 'question'. If you say 'there is no question that Ben Jonson was in Edinburgh in 1618' most people, perhaps all, will take you to mean that he *was* there in that year; and the same if you say 'that Jonson was in Edinburgh in 1618 is beyond question' or 'does not admit of question'. If, however, you say that 'there is no question of Jonson having been in Edinburgh in 1618', most people, though I think not all, will take you to mean that he was *not* there in that year. But there is certainly no question that it would be better

to use a phrase the meaning of which is not open to question.

Avoid also the word 'doubtless', which has been defined as 'a word used when making a statement for the truth of which the speaker is unaware of any evidence'.

Do not overtask such expressions as 'it is generally admitted that', 'there can be no doubt that', 'it is well known that' unless you can shift your responsibility on to at least one other person by giving a reference.

9. Always be precise and careful in references and quotations, and never fear the charge of pedantry. After all, 'pedant' is merely the name which one gives to anyone whose standard of accuracy happens to be a little higher than one's own!

10. Do not treat the subjects of your research with levity. Above all avoid that hateful back-slapping 'heartiness' which caused certain nineteenth-century Elizabethans to refer to 'Tom Nash', 'Bob Green', 'Will Shakespeare' and so on, with its horrible flavour of modern gutter journalism which refers in this way to film stars, long-distance fliers, and the like. These Elizabethans had certain qualities which have made it seem worth while to keep their memories green for more than 300 years, and on this account, if for no other, they should be given the courtesy which is their due.

11. Above all, whatever inner doubts you may have as to whether the piece of research upon which you have been spending your time was really worth while, you must on no account allow it to appear that you have ever thought of it otherwise than of supreme importance to the human race! In the first place, unless you yourself believe in what you are doing, you will certainly not do good work, and, secondly, if your reader suspects for a moment that you do not set the very highest value on your work yourself he will set no value on it at all. He will on the other hand be full of fury that you should have induced him to waste his precious time in reading stuff that you do not believe in yourself, an attitude which will completely prevent him from appreciating any real and evident merit which there may be in it. After all, one can

never be certain of the value of one's own work. Often in scientific research a discovery which in itself seemed most trivial has led to results of the utmost importance, and though sensational occurrences of this kind may be rarer in literary research than in science, it is still true that what is merely a side-issue in one research may give rise, when critically examined, to results of quite unexpected value.

As a general rule the interest and importance of a piece of research lies either in the facts disclosed or the methods by which they have been brought to light—or in both. To these prior considerations the manner of presentation may indeed be subordinate. Nevertheless good presentation may help enormously in the effective value of good research, while bad presentation may rob it of the recognition which is its due.

William Riley Parker and others

8.   *The MLA style sheet**

Scholarship and Readability

Readability is a prime consideration of scholarly writing. American scholarship over the past quarter century has moved away from fact gathering for its own sake and a system of annotation virtually independent of the text. Prose is more pleasant to read if it does not require one to jump constantly to the foot of the page or to the back of the book. Every effort should be made to make the text self sufficient, to make the annotation unobtrusive, and to consolidate footnote references. Yet scholarship will continue to differ from the personal essay in that its facts and inferences are fully documented. Successful scholarly writing achieves that most difficult feat of blending maximum interest and readability with maximum accuracy and evidence. In presenting his documentation economically the writer must depend upon the perception of his reader. We hope that the first edition of the *MLA Style Sheet* may take some credit for having increased the sophistication

* From *The MLA Style Sheet* (New York: Modern Language Association of America, 1951, revised 1970), paragraphs 1–22. This advice is designed for the preparation of books and scholarly articles, but applies largely to the preparation of a typed thesis as well, though variations are permissible. The *Style Sheet* is kept under revision by *MLA* in consultation with learned journals and university presses. Its second half (paragraphs 213–44) consists of sample footnotes, abbreviations, advice about proof reading, etc.

of a generation of readers, as well as for having encouraged the use of a uniform system of annotation whose conventions make possible compression without loss of comprehension.

Preparing the Manuscript

1. In general, type your manuscript to meet the practical needs of your editor and printer, as directed in Sections 2–6, below. Do not try to make your manuscript look like printed pages, unless you receive special instructions from your editor or supervisor (as for dissertations). (If the pages are to be photographed, you may be asked to observe special margins, to single space quotations, and to type the notes at the foot of the page. This will usually involve double typing or other special procedures on your part.) Cooperate with learned journals and presses by submitting copy in finished form, appropriate for printing. Poor copy not only wastes the editor's time but also, since it takes longer to set in type, increases the printer's bill. Authors should always copyread carefully before sending off a manuscript, whether or not they do their own typing, and should check all quotations and references against the originals, never waiting for galley proofs as a basis for checking.

2. Paper. Type on one side only of good, white paper $8\frac{1}{2}$ x 11 inches in size (8 x 10 inches in most of Europe). Use twenty-pound bond; avoid 'erasable' paper, which will not take corrections in ink, and never use thin paper unless for your carbon. A carbon or photo copy with all corrections inserted, and numbered exactly like the original, should always be retained by the author when the original is sent away.[1]

3. Typing. The article or book should be typed with DOUBLE SPACING throughout, including footnotes or endnotes and quotations of prose or verse intended to be set in reduced type. Foot-

---

[1] Some journals do not return the original with galley proof, but assume that the author has retained a corrected copy.

notes, which are usually set separately and not positioned until paging, should be typed with DOUBLE SPACING (triple spacing between notes) on separate sheets following the last page of the article (or chapter of the book). A fresh typewriter ribbon and clean type will contribute greatly to the legibility of copy. *Never* fasten the pages together with more than a paper clip.

4. Margins. Consistently leave margins of from 1 to 1½ inches at the top, bottom, and sides, particularly the left-hand side. The editor needs this space for his instructions to the printer or queries to you, and regular margins enable him better to estimate the length which the article or book will have in print.

5. Pagination. Number pages consecutively throughout the entire manuscript (including notes) in the upper right corner, or centered at the top, after the manuscript is in final form. If you have numbered while typing and have later been forced to insert 15a, 15b, or to number a page 15–16 to show a page deleted, renumber consecutively in pencil or ink on both original and carbon before submitting the manuscript. Typing your last name before the number on each page is good insurance against the misplacing of pages in editorial handling.

6. Corrections and insertions. If they are brief, type or write them legibly, in ink, above the line involved. Never use the margins or write below the line. Make no unnecessary marks (e.g. proofreading symbols should not be used). If corrections are lengthy, you may type them, as inserts, on separate, full-sized pages, clearly marking them (e.g. "Insert A, page —"); numbering each to follow the page to which it makes a contribution, and indicating exactly in the manuscript itself, with an arrow and a circled note in the margin, where it is to go. Better still, retype and submit a clean copy even if there are some short pages.

7. Signature (articles). For your own safety and for your editor's convenience, type in the upper *left* corner of the first page of your text, not on a separate page, your name and the address to which you want the manuscript returned or proof sent. If a future address, temporary or permanent, is definitely known to you, give it also, with pertinent dates. The style of most journals requires, moreover, that the author's name (as he wishes it to appear) be typed below the title of his article, and that his formal academic address be typed at the end of the article, not the end of the notes, on the left-hand side. However, since journals have different styles for signatures, ascertain the style of the journal to which you are submitting your manuscript. It is a courtesy, which will not go unobserved, to retype your first page and possibly the last when submitting to a second or third journal, making the signature conform to its particular style.

8. Titles. For articles, unlike books, type the title two or three inches from the top of the page on which the text begins—not on a separate page. *Do not underline your title or capitalize it in full.* (See Sec. 16c below.) Underline only a published work, or a word in an etymological study, mentioned in it. Do not use a period after titles or any centered headings. The title should not carry a reference to a footnote, unless by your editor; in articles put necessary acknowledgements or explanations in a footnote to the first or last sentence.

9. Type faces. Indicate *italics* by a single underline; SMALL CAPITALS, by two underlines, LARGE CAPITALS, by typing ordinary capitals (or by three underlines below small letters); *ITALIC LARGE CAPITALS*, by a single underline below typed capitals (or by four underlines below small letters); **boldface type,** by a wavy underline, inserted by hand. Double or triple underlining is also better done with a pen than attempted on the typewriter. In linguistic studies it is often advisable to do even single underlining by hand after the manuscript has been typed, for typed underlines may cut through the bottoms of the letters *g j p q y* and interefere seriously with the addition of diacritics below the letters.

The Text

10. Textual divisions. Avoid formal divisions of short articles. If, however, you separate related groups of paragraphs by skipping four lines, you can leave the decision to your editor. In long articles, related groups of paragraphs may be numbered (usually with Roman numerals) and the first paragraph of each group, when it seems appropriate, preceded by a subtitle centered or flush with the left margin. A series of topics, arguments, or conclusions may be briefly stated with numbers in column.

II. Paragraphs. For the sake of both appearance and emphasis, avoid writing many very short or very long paragraphs, especially in sequence. Remember that brief paragraphs on your typed page will look even briefer in print. Short paragraphs may, of course, acquire virtue in articles intended for journals which print in two columns.

12. Titles in text. After the first full reference, usually in a note, consistently use short (if possible, familiar) titles or abbreviations when the same works are mentioned often in your text. Enclose in quotation marks (do not underline) titles of articles, essays, short stories, short poems, chapters and sections of books, and unpublished works such as dissertations. Underline titles of published books, plays, long poems, pamphlets, periodicals, and classical works (except books of the Bible). The above conventions do not apply to names of series or societies or editions; leave them in roman, without quotes. On capitalization see Secs. 16*c–h*.

13. Quotations. *a.* In general, all quotations should correspond exactly with the originals in wording, spelling, and interior punctuation. The first word of a quotation that is a complete sentence and that is not grammatically a part of another sentence should begin with a capital. Conversely, if the quotation is run into a text sentence, the first word should not be capitalized even though it is capitalized in the original. Other exceptions (e.g., the italicizing of words for emphasis, or the modernizing of spelling) should be explicitly indicated or explained. For terminal punctuation see Sec. 14*i*.

b. Ellipsis. For ellipsis within a sentence, use three . . . *spaced* periods, being careful to leave a space before the first period. Quotations that are complete sentences should end with periods even though matter that was within the original may have been omitted. To indicate ellipsis after the conclusion of a complete sentence, use three spaced periods *in addition* to the sentence period. . . . —i.e., four periods with no space before the first. All punctuation except this end stop period should be ignored when it falls within an ellipsis. If the extent of the omission is significant, indicate an ellipsis of one whole line (or more) in a verse quotation, or of a whole paragraph (or more) in a prose quotation, by a single typed line of spaced periods; otherwise, simply use three spaced periods after the last word before the ellipsis. Avoid using spaced periods to open or to close obviously incomplete quotations (e.g., a phrase or a dependent clause). Use introductory clauses to avoid opening paragraphs with ellipsis periods (Gibson observes that "while Mark Twain," etc.).

c. Interpolations. Interpolation of your own comment or explanation in quoted matter is permissible if enclosed in square brackets (never parentheses) which you may have to put it by hand. Use "sic"—sparingly—in square brackets to assure the reader that you are quoting accurately although the spelling or logic might otherwise lead him to doubt it.

d. Poetry. Unless unusual emphasis is required, verse quotations of a single line or part of a line should be run on, in quotation marks, as part of your text. Quotations of two lines *may* be run on in quotation marks also, but with the lines separated by a slash (/): e.g., see 13*g*, below. When not run on, verse quotations should be separated from the context (for setting in reduced type), introduced (in most instances) by a colon, centered on the page, and typed with double spacing but with quotation marks omitted, unless they occur in the original.

e. Prose. A quotation of less than 100 words set in reduced type makes an unpleasing page, and a run-on quotation of 100 words or more tends to make the reader lose track of the context. Therefore, unless special emphasis is required, prose quotations up to 100 words in any language should always be run on, in quotation marks (except for languages in non-Roman alphabets) as part of your text. In such cases, when beginning and ending quotation marks are used, subquotes within the excerpt may need to be adjusted, i.e., reduced from double to single quotation marks.

Longer quotations (100 words or more) should be separated from the context, not enclosed in quotation marks but marked in some way for setting in reduced type (e.g., by a neat vertical line inserted by hand, along the left margin of the matter quoted, or by typing with slight indention on the left margin—not by single spacing). If a single paragraph, or part of one, is quoted, do not indent the first line; but if two or more paragraphs are quoted consecutively, indent the first line of each. Use a colon when a quotation is formally introduced (e.g., when your preceding sentence has said or implied something about the quotation), but not when a quotation is an integral element of your sentence. Since quotations separated from the context are not set off by quotation marks, interior punctuation is not affected.

f. Permissions. It is difficult to generalize about this matter. The length of a quotation is not normally the determining factor. Many publishers require permissions for short quotations, particularly of modern poetry, or if the matter is substantive (e.g., an apothegm). Fifty-three members of the Association of American University Presses have adopted a "Resolution on Permissions" that allows "scholars to quote without permission from published sources whatever they legitimately need to make their scholarly writings complete, accurate, and authenticated": "We the undersigned members of the Association of American University Presses agree as follows: 1. That publications issued under our imprints may be quoted without specific prior permission in works of original scholarship for accurate citation of authority or for criticism, review, or evaluation, subject to the conditions listed below. 2. That appropriate credit be given in the case of each quotation. 3. That waiver of the requirement for specific permission does not extend to quotations that are complete units in themselves (as poems, letters, short stories, essays, journal articles, complete chapters or sections of books, maps, charts, graphs, tables, drawings, or other illustrative materials), in whatever form they may be reproduced; nor does the waiver extend to quotation of whatever length presented as primary material for its own sake (as in anthologies or books of readings). 4. The fact that specific permission for quoting materials may be waived under this agreement does not relieve the quoting author and publisher from the responsibility of determining 'fair use' of such material." Sixty-eight journals in the humanities have subscribed to a similar statement. The revision of the U.S. Copyright Law now pending before Congress provides that the "fair use of a copyrighted work ... for purposes such as criticism, comment, news reporting, teaching, scholarship, or research, is not an infringement of copyright." Permission to quote should be requested, when necessary, from the holder of the copyright. Particularly when quoting from scholarly journals, it is a courtesy to request permission also from the author if the copyright holder does not do so. When requesting permission to quote (or reprint articles or sections of books), authors should give full and accurate reference to the material involved and specify the intended use of the material (method of publication, publisher, intended audience, size of edition, etc.). The copyright period in the United States is currently twenty-eight years with provision for renewal for a second period of twenty-eight years.

g. Citing references. Insert reference numbers at the end of any quoted material; or, if the source is clearly indicated and has been fully cited previously, omit the footnote and give the exact page (or line, or volume and page) reference in parentheses immediately after the quotation; for example: Many a note-taking scholar, like Milton's Satan, "through the armed files / Darts his experienced eye" (1.567–568). Put this parenthetical reference after the quotation marks but before the comma or period when the quotation is part of your text—after all punctuation when it is set off by different type (or single spacing in theses).

h. Parallel texts. Use sequence only for short, scattered comparisons. In an article, extended parallels of two or more texts should be arranged in columns, with alignment clearly indicated; in a book, they may be arranged on facing pages.

i. Quotation marks. See Sec. 14*i*, below.

14. Punctuation. *a.* In general, make your usage as consistent as possible. Although the finer points of punctuation are often a matter of personal preference, the main purpose is clarity, and of this someone else can often judge better than you.

b. Commas. Use them before "and" and "or" in a series of three of more. Never use a comma and a dash together. The comma follows a parenthesis (such as this), if the context requires a comma.

c. Dashes. A dash is typed as two hyphens, with no blank space before or after—*not* one hyphen between two spaces. See Sec. 25 for a use of the dash in documentation.

d. Exclamation marks should be used sparingly in scholarly writing.

e. Hyphens. Avoid ending a typed line with a hyphen which is to be printed, for the compositor may drop the hyphen and join the two parts in one. Instead, sacrifice appearance and put the entire compound on the next line.

f. Periods end footnote citations as well as complete sentences in text and notes. On ellipsis, see Sec. 13*b*.

g. Square brackets, to be inserted by hand if they are not on your typewriter, are used for an unavoidable parenthesis within a parenthesis, to enclose interpolations in a quotation or in incomplete data, and to enclose phonetic transcription. (Slash marks are used to enclose phonemic transcriptions.)

h. Words discussed. Enclose in double quotation marks words to which attention is being directed (e.g., slang, words purposely misused, words used as words) and English translations of words or phrases from a foreign language. But in *linguistic* studies underline, do not quote, all linguistic forms (words, phrases, letters) cited as examples or as subjects of discussion, whether English or foreign; and use single quotation marks for definitions or translations, without intervening punctuation (e.g., *ainsi* 'thus').

i. Quotations. For quotations run on as part of your text, first use double quotation marks, then, for quotations within quotations, single marks. For the sake of appearance put all commas or periods *inside* quotation marks unless a parenthetical reference intervenes (e.g., see Sec. 13*g*, above) or unless exact reproduction of punctuation is of peculiar significance (as in bibliographical description). Other punctuation goes inside quotation marks only when it is actually part of the matter quoted.

15. Numerals. *a. In general*, numbers of fewer than three digits should be spelled out except in technical or statistical discussions involving their frequent use, or in footnotes, where many space-saving devices are legitimate. If Arabic numerals are used for numbers over 99, use them also for smaller numbers in the same sentence or related groups of sentences. Never use capital "I" for the Arabic numeral one. If your typewriter does not have "1", use small "l." Dates and page numbers are rarely spelled out: "1 April" and "page 2" are preferable to "the first of April" and "the second page". Numbers beginning sentences (including dates) are always spelled out.

b. Dates. Consistently follow these examples: "17 August 1951" (*PMLA* style) or "August 17, 1951," but not both styles (if the latter, use a comma both before and after the year); "August 1951" or "August, 1951," but not both; "March 2, 1625/6" to indicate both the legal and calendar year in dates from January 1 to March 25; "3 November 1963 (K'ang hsi 32/10/6)" to indicate both European and non-European dates; "1880s" but "eighties"; "in 1951–52" or "from 1951 to 1952," but not "from 1951–52"; "500 B.C." but "A.D. 500." In your text spell out references to centuries, e.g., "seventeenth-century spelling persisted into the eighteenth century."

c. Inclusive numbers. In connecting consecutive numbers, give the second number in full for numbers through 999; for larger numbers give only two figures of the second if it is within the same hundred, e.g., pp. 21–28, 345–346, 1608–74, 12345–47.

d. Roman numerals. Use capitals for book, volume, act, part, division, or individual in a series (as Henry VIII). Use lower case for chapters, preliminary pages, scenes, cantos, etc. When in doubt use lower case, for, if wrong, "ix" is more easily corrected by your editor than is "IX."

16. Spelling. *a. Spelling.* including hyphenation, must be consistent, except in quotations, of course. Use one dictionary throughout; Webster's is standard for American spelling, Oxford for English. Most American journals prefer American usage.

b. Apostrophe. Form the possessive of *monosyllabic* proper names ending in *s* or another sibilant by adding an apostrophe and *s* (e.g., Keats's poems, Marx's theories) except, by convention, for ancient classical names (e.g., Mars' wrath). In words of more than one syllable ending in a sibilant, add the apostrophe only (e.g., Hopkins' poems, Ceres' rites) except for names ending in a sibilant and final *e* (e.g., Horace's odes). See also *Webster's New Collegiate Dictionary* s.v. "possessive."

c. Capitalization—English. Capitalize the first letter of the first word and of all the principal words—including nouns and proper adjectives in hyphenated compounds, but not articles, prepositions, and conjunctions—in English titles of publications, in divisions of works, and in subjects of lectures or papers; but in mentioning magazines or newspapers (e.g., the *Gentleman's Magazine*), do not treat an initial definite article as part of the title except when the name is cited separately as a source, e.g., in a list or bibliography. Capitalize references to parts of a specific work, e.g., Morley's Preface and Index. Capitalize and, in documentation, abbreviate a noun followed by a numeral indicating place in a sequence, e.g., Vol. II of 3 vols., Pl. 4, No. 20, Act V, Ch. iii, Version A—but not fol., l., n., p., or sig. Never capitalize entire words (i.e., every letter) in titles cited in text or notes.

d. Capitalization—French. In prose or poetry French differs from English usage in that the following are not capitalized unless they begin a sentence or (in some cases) a line of poetry: a) the subject pronoun *je* (I); b) days of the week or months; c) names of languages and adjectives derived from proper nouns; d) titles of people or places. (Examples: Un Français m'a parlé en anglais dans la place de la Concorde. Hier j'ai vu le docteur Maurois qui conduisait une voiture Ford. Le capitaine Boutillier m'a dit qu'il partait pour Rouen le premier jeudi d'avril avec quelques amis normands.) In titles of books, stories, poems, etc., capitalize the first word and all proper nouns. If the first word is an article, capitalize also the first noun and any preceding adjectives. (Examples: *Du côté de chez Swann. Le Grand Meaulnes. La Guerre de Troie n'aura pas lieu.*) In titles of series and periodicals, capitalize all major words. (Examples: *La Revue des Deux Mondes. L'Ami du Peuple.*)

   e. *Capitalization—German.* In prose or poetry German differs from English usage in that the following are not capitalized unless they begin a sentence or, usually, a line of poetry: a) the subject pronoun *ich* (I); b) days of the week or names of languages used adjectively or adverbially; c) adjectives derived from proper nouns, except that those derived from personal names are capitalized when they refer explicitly to the works and deeds of those persons. (Examples: Ein französischer Schriftsteller, den ich gut kenne, arbeitet sonntags immer an seinem neuen Buch über die platonische Liebe. *Der Staat* ist eine von den bekanntesten Platonischen Schriften.) Always capitalized in German are: a) the pronoun *Sie* (you) and its possessive *Ihr* (your), and their inflected forms; b) all substantives, including adjectives, infinitives, pronouns, prepositions, etc., when used substantively; c) adjectives derived from personal names when referring explicitly to the works and deeds of those persons (see c above); d) adjectives derived from the names of cities with the addition of the suffix *-er*; e) ordinal numerals used in titles; f) attributive adjectives used in titles of persons. (Examples: Fahren Sie mit Ihrer Frau zurück? Ich glaube an das Gute in der Welt. Er schreibt, nur um dem Auf und Ab der Buch-Nachfrage zu entsprechen. Die Einsteinsche Relativitätstheorie; die Berliner Luft: der Zweite Weltkrieg; Karl der Grosse.) In letters and ceremonial writings, the pronouns *du* and *ihr* (you) and their derivatives are capitalized. In titles of books, stories, poems, etc., capitalize the first word;

otherwise follow the rules of usage set forth above. (Examples: *Ein treuer Diener seines Herrn. Thomas Mann und die Grenzen des Ich*.) In titles of series and periodicals, capitalize all major words. (Example: *Zeitschrift für Vergleichende Sprachforschung*.)

f. Capitalization—Italian. In prose or poetry Italian differs from English usage in that the following are not capitalized unless they begin a sentence or, usually, a line of poetry: a) the subject pronoun *io* (I); b) days of the week or months; c) names of languages and adjectives derived from proper nouns; d) titles of people or places. But centuries and other large divisions of time are capitalized. (Examples: Un Italiano parlava francese con uno Svizzero in piazza di Spagna. Il dottor Bruno ritornerò dall'Italia giovedì otto agosto e io partirò il nove. La lirica del Novecento. Il Rinascimento.) In all titles, the prevailing contemporary usage is to capitalize only the first word and names or persons and places. (Examples: *Dizionario letterario Bompiani. Bibliografia della critica pirandelliana. L'arte tipografica in Urbino. Collezione di classici italiani. Studi petrarcheschi*.)

g. Capitalization—Portuguese. In prose or poetry Portuguese differs from English usage in that the following are not capitalized unless they begin a sentence or (at times) a line of poetry: a) the subject pronoun *eu* (I); b) days of the week; c) names of the months in Brazil (they are capitalized in Portugal); d) adjectives derived from proper names; e) titles of people and places in Portugal (they are capitalized in Brazil); f) points of the compass when indicating direction (ao norte de América) but capitalized when indicating regions (os americanos do Norte). Brazilian Portuguese capitalizes nouns used abstractly to refer to concepts, institutions, or branches of knowledge (a Igreja, a Nação, a Matemática). (Examples, *Peninsular usage:* Vi o doutor Silva na praça de República. A marinha americana. *Brazilian usage:* O francês falava da Historia do Brasil na Praça Tiradentes, utilizando o inglés. Ontem eu vi o Doutor Garcia, aquêle que tem un carro Ford. Então me disse Dona Teresa que pretendia sair para o Recife a primeira segunda-feira de abril com alguns amigos mineiros.) In titles of books, stories, poems, etc., majority usage capitalizes only the first word and names of person and places. (Examples: *A bico do pena. O espirito das leis. Problemas da linguagem e do estilo.*) Minority usage capitalizes all major words. (Examples: *As Viagens do Infante Dom Pedro as Quatro Partes do Mundo. Gabriela, Cravo e Canela.*) In series, journal and newspaper titles, capitalize all major words. (Examples: *Boletim de Filologia. Revista Lusitana. Correo da Manhã.*)

h. Capitalization—Spanish. In prose or poetry, Spanish differs from English usage in that the following are not capitalized unless they begin a sentence or, sometimes, a line of poetry: a) the subject pronoun *yo* (I); b) days of the week or months; c) nouns or adjectives derived from proper nouns; d) titles of people or places. (Examples: El francés hablaba inglés en la plaza Colón. Ayer yo vi al doctor García que manejaba un couche Ford. Me dijo don Jorge que iba a salir para Sevilla el primer martes de abril con unos amigos neoyorkinos.) In titles of books, stories, poems, etc., capitalize only the first word and names of persons and places. (Examples: *Historia verdadera de la conquista de la Nueva España. La gloria de don Ramiro. Extremos de América. Trasmundo de Goya. Breve historia del ensayo hispanoamericano.*) In series, journal and newspaper titles, the predominant usage is to capitalize all major words. (Examples: *Revista de Filologia Española. Biblioteca de Autores Españoles. Fichero Bibliográfico Hispanoamericano. El Mercurio. La Nación. La Prensa.*) A minority usage treats series and journal titles like book titles. (Examples: *Revista de filologia española,* Biblioteca de autores españoles.)

i. Italics. Avoid frequent use of underlining for emphasis. But underline names of ships, titles of published books, plays, pamphlets, periodicals, and long poems (see Sec. 12, above), words or phrases cited as linguistic examples, and foreign words used in an English text (except quotations, titles of articles, proper names, and foreign words anglicized through usage).[1]

---

[1] Since the American language rapidly naturalizes foreign words, especially in certain periods or among certain large groups of people, the writer needs both

j. Accents. In French words typed entirely in capitals, accent only E and U. Do not accent capitals followed by lower case or small caps.

k. Dieresis. In German words use it (not *e*) for umlaut, even for initial capitals (e.g., Uber). But in English text observe common usage for names, e.g., Goethe but Göttingen.

l. Ligature. Unless you have ligatures on your typewriter, indicate them on your manuscript by a curved line, made by hand, joining the tops of the two letters, e.g., French oe for œ, German *sz* for ß (preferably written so by hand), Old English ae for æ. Except when quoting, do not use ligatures in Latin, Greek, or modern English words, e.g., Oedipus, aetatis, aesthetic (or esthetic), mediaeval (or medieval).

m. Latin. Except in texts or linguistic studies, ordinarily differentiate *u* and *v*, *i* and *j*.

17. Names of persons. Since there are exceptions to almost any rules that can be formulated, good judgment based on knowledge of common usage is essential. Here are some of the problems. Because formal titles (Mr., Mrs., Dr., Professor, etc.) are usually omitted in references to prominent persons, living or dead, it is often an implied compliment to omit them in references to fellow scholars or critics—but sometimes not when attacking, or making personal comment, or acknowledging assistance. By convention, titles are associated with or used for certain eminent names, e.g., Surrey (i.e., Henry Howard, Earl of Surrey), Lord Byron, Dr. Johnson (but cf. Tennyson and Browne). "Miss" and "Mrs." may be politely omitted in many instances, especially if replaced by a given name, e.g., Emily Dickinson, Marjorie Nicolson, Louise Pound (but cf. Mrs. Browning. Mme de Staël, Cather). Simplified names of famous authors are common and acceptable

knowledge and judgment to apply this convention; dictionaries, which used to assist him, are beginning to abandon a labeling which can soon become out of date. Much depends, in any case, upon the writer's audience. No matter what the audience, the scholarly author does not italicize such words as "cliché," "enjambement," "genre," "hubris," "leitmotif," and "mimesis."

(e.g., Dante, Voltaire), as are pseudonyms (George Eliot, Anatole France, Gorki), but foreign names can often present problems to the uninitiated. For example, French *de* and Spanish *de* and German *von* and Dutch *van der* are used following a given name, but not (with some exceptions, e.g., De Gaulle) with the last name alone. A hyphen is normally used between French given names (e.g., M.-J. Sue is Marie-Joseph, known to readers as "Eugène" Sue but M. R. Canat is Monsieur René Canat). German names with an umlaut (ä, ö, ü) are alphabetized as though spelled out (*ae*, *oe*, *ue*). Spanish names can be the most troublesome of all; they may consist of one or two given names, plus a paternal name, plus a maternal name—the last two with or without the conjunction *y*—and with alphabetizing or reference depending upon whether or not the paternal or maternal name is considered "weak" (i.e., commonplace, undistinguished). Increasing the confusion for foreigners, many Spanish names are contracted; thus, one must somehow learn how properly to index or refer to Juan de *Valdés*, Federico García *Lorca*, Vicente *Blasco Ibáñez*, and José *Ortega y Gasset*. In French and Spanish, when the preposition *de* and the definite article are combined in a single word (*du*, *del*, *des*), this word must be used with the last name; Bertrand *Du Guesclin*, Guillaume *Du Vair*, Guillermo *Del Olmo*, Angel *Del Río*, le chevalier *Des Grieux*, Bonaventure *Des Perriers*. Otherwise, omit *de* with last name: Étienne de *La Boétie*, Jean de *La Bruyère*, Bartolomé de *Las Casas*. In Chinese, Japanese, Korean, and Vietnamese, surnames precede given names (Hu Shih, Wang Kuo-wei, Anesaki Masaharu), but Western authors should follow the known preferences of Oriental scholars or public figures, even if they differ from normal practice or standard romanization (e.g., Y. R. Chao, Chiang Kai-shek, Daisetz Suzuki). Some surnames are almost inseparable from initials ("O. Henry," H. G. Wells); others, from the given names ("Mark Twain," Amy Lowell).

18. Transliteration. The following observations are intended more to call attention to the problems than to offer definitive solutions. Authors working on subjects that involve either non-Roman characters or transliteration would do well, before final typing, to consult prospective editors about their special requirements.[1]

a. Russian, Mongolian, and Korean. In transliteration of Russian follow the system used by the Library of Congress; on Mongolian, the system in Antoine Mostaert, *Dictionnaire ordos*, III (Peking: The Catholic Univ., 1944), 769–809; of Korean, the McCune-Reischauer system in "The Romanization of the Korean Language," *Transactions of the Korean Branch, Royal Asiatic Society*, 29 (1939), 1–55. J. Thomas Shaw, *The Transliteration of Modern Russian for English Language Publications* (Madison: Univ. of Wisconsin Press, 1967), provides a thorough discussion of various systems.

b. Chinese and Japanese. For Chinese, use the modified Wade-Giles system as given in "List of Syllabic Headings" in the American edition of Mathews' *Chinese-English Dictionary* (Cambridge: Harvard Univ. Press, 1943), pp. xviii–xxi, omitting the circumflex and breve but retaining the umlaut *ü*. For well-known place names use the established forms, e.g., Yang-tze, Nanking, Fukien, following the system in the China Postal Atlas (Nanking: Directorate General of Posts, 1933); for others use Wade-Giles with hyphens between the elements. In general, hyphenate transcribed Chinese forms to achieve meaningful units, e.g., *shih-hsüeh yen-chiu*. For Japanese, use the romanization system of Kenkyusha's *New Japanese-English Dictionary*, the 1942 edition (Cambridge: Harvard Univ. Press), but use an apostrophe after *n* at the end of a syllable if followed by a vowel or *y* (Gen'e, San'yo). Use macrons over long vowels in all but well-known place names (Kyoto, Hokkaido) and anglicized Japanese words (shogun, Daimyo). Use hyphens sparingly (*Meiji jidai shi no shinkenkyu*).

---

[1] The Chicago Press *Manual of Style*, 12th ed. (1969), pp. 213–34, contains a full discussion of the special problems of editing, composing in, and transliterating various foreign languages.

c. Indonesian, Malay, and other Southeast Asian languages. Follow the system given in John M. Echols and Hassan Shadily, *Indonesian-English Dictionary*, 2nd ed. (Ithaca: Cornell Univ. Press, 1963). In the absence of a single standard form for Thai or Burmese, and in view of the problem of diacritics for Vietnamese, follow any consistent, intelligible form for these languages, but avoid diacritics not in general use for other languages. For Tagalog, follow the system given in *A National Language-English Vocabulary*, published by the Institute of National Language (Manila, 1950).

d. Sanskrit and Hindi. For Sanskrit the standard system is given in A. L. Basham, *The Wonder That Was India* (New York: Grove Press, 1959), Appendix 10. (This coincides with most earlier systems except that the palatal sibilant is rendered as ś.) Give the stem form to nouns used in an English sentence (e.g., "the *dharma* of the king"). Deviations should be left unitalicized, e.g., "the Brahmin priests," but "the *brāhmana* priests." In transliteration of Hindi the Sanskrit syllabic *r* (*Krsna*) becomes *ri* (*Krisna*), and the following symbols in addition to those given in Basham are recommended: *q* (voiceless post-velar stop), *x* (voiceless post-velar fricative), *z* (voiced alveolar groove fricative), *f* (voiceless labio-dental fricative), and *g* (voiced post-velar fricative).

e. Hebrew. In transliterating Hebrew, use the Sephardi (Israeli) pronunciation in determining transliteration, and the system set forth in the *Style Manual of the U.S. Government Printing Office* (Washington D.C.: U.S. Government Printing Office, 1967), pp. 428–33. Although Hebrew uses no capitals, in transliteration capitalize initial letters of proper names and all words used in titles, e.g., ha-Olam. (The article should, however, be capitalized if it is part of the first word in the title.) Yiddish, which employs the same alphabet, should be transliterated phonetically, with special care to distinguish its spelling from that of German.

f. Languages using Arabic script. Use the transliteration tables approved by the Library of Congress and the American Library Association and published as bulletins of the U.S. Library of Congress, Processing Department, Cataloging Service. Bulletin

49 (Nov. 1958), Arabic; Bull. 59 (July 1963), Persian; Bull. 64 (Feb. 1964), Languages of India, and Pakistan, except Kashmiri, Sindhi, Pushto; Bull. 716 (July 1965), Pushto; Bull. 76 (Oct. 1966), Languages of Burma and Thailand. Capitalization should be employed as in English save that the article *al* is in lower case in all positions (Abd al-Husayn, Nizām al-Din). In cases where the original publication includes a transliteration of the author's name, this should be included as a subentry after the accurate transliteration, and, of course, familiar place names should be used in preference to unfamiliar transliterated forms: Tehran, Kabul, Peshawar, Tihrān, Kābul, Peshāwar.

g. Modern Greek. For modern and classical Greek use the transliteration tables approved by the Library of Congress and the American Library Association, printed in *A. L. A. Cataloging Rules for Author and Title Entries* (Chicago: American Library Association, 1949). In Greek books, the author's name appears on the title page in the genitive case (Hypo [by] Perikleous Alexandrou Argyropoulou). When name is cited, the first name and surname are nominative. The second or patronymic remains genitive because it means "son of" (Perikles Alexandrou Argyropoulos). Women's names are cited, first name nominative, patronymic and surname both genitive (Aikaterine Geōrgiou Koumarianou).

h. Use of characters. In general, although characters may be added to transliterations (e.g., from Chinese or Japanese), they should be used only when important in facilitating identification, never for words or names which are well-known or readily identified. An English translation after the romanized title of a book or article will often make the addition of characters unnecessary.

19. Cross references. For unavoidable cross references to passages in the text of your own article or book, never type the page numbers of your manuscript but use two or three ciphers as in the formula, "See above (or below), p. 000." Such references cannot be completed until page proof, and either blank spaces or actual numbers that have to be changed later are very easily overlooked. On the other hand, be certain to assist your editor by giving *in the margin*, circled, the exact page of your manuscript, and in the margin of that page a circled confirming note, e.g., "ref. for fn. 17, p. 27." Most journals submit only galley proof to authors.

Documentation

20. In general, citation of sources for statements of fact or opinion, or for quoted matter, should be kept as concise as the demands of clarity and complete accuracy permit. If the reference is brief, insert it, within parentheses, in the text itself (see Sec. 13*g*); if it is lengthy, put it in a note. Let the test be whether or not it interferes seriously with ease in reading, remembering that the footnote number, which teases the reader to look at the bottom of the page,[1] may be more of an interruption than such a simple reference in your text as (II, 241) or (p. 72). Your first full reference to a work from which you intend to quote a number of times should usually be in a note, but you may say there that subsequent references to this edition will appear in your text. Avoid large numbers of very short notes. Except for glosses, definitions, and incomplete quotations introduced by three periods, footnotes should begin with capitals and end with periods. Footnotes are intended to be read like sentences, without internal full stops (hence the enclosure of place of publication and publisher in parentheses, whereas in bibliographies they are set off by periods).

21. Footnote logic. The conventions of documentation are largely means to an end, to enable the reader to follow up your sources with ease. Hence, the footnote number in the text should come as near to the beginning of "borrowed" material as is conveniently possible, though always at the end of a direct quotation. But annotate only where there is a reason. For example, it is rarely necessary to give references for proverbs or familiar quotations (e.g., "stilus virum arguit"), or to give line references

---

[1] Like this. And suppose you had found only "Ibid."

for short poems (e.g., sonnets), or to spell out the full names of familiar authors, or to give page references to works alphabetically arranged. To do such things—and to omit *dates* of works or events discussed—is to forget the reader and think only of the machinery of scholarship. Information given in your text need not be repeated in a footnote; hence many notes can easily be shortened or avoided by taking the trouble to give *complete* titles or dates or names of authors in the text itself. Essay-like notes that pursue separate arguments are bad form. Exposition that cannot be accommodated in the text should be omitted. Successive quotations in one paragraph may usually be documented in a single note, and "covering footnotes" may be used to acknowledge general sources, thereby avoiding a series of citations. E.g., "Howarth, p. xxi. I follow throughout Howarth's meticulous account of the sources." In references to classics of which many editions are available and the nature of which makes line citations impractical, it is often helpful to give the reader more information than the page number of the edition used, e.g., "p. 271 (Bk. IV, Ch. ii)."

22. Footnote numbers. Footnotes should be numbered consecutively, starting from 1, throughout an article or review or chapter of a book unless a special section, such as an annotated text or numerical tables, requires a separate series. Never number by pages, for this necessitates renumbering when the work is set in type. Do not use asterisks or other symbols; use Arabic numbers, and type them exactly as they are to appear in print, without such embellishments as periods, parentheses, or slashes (which would have to be deleted by your editor). Footnote numbers are "superior figures"; in your text type them slightly above the line, always *after* the punctuation, if any, and always after a quotation—not after the author's name or the introductory verb or the colon preceding quoted matter. In the note itself, indent the first line five spaces, type the footnote number without punctuation, skip a space, and begin the reference. The footnote numbers as well as the references should be verified before the manuscript is submitted. *Footnotes themselves should be typed double spaced.*

Acknowledgements

We are grateful to the following for permission to reproduce copyright material:

Cambridge University Press for 'English Collectors' from *English Collectors of Books and Manuscripts 1530–1930* by Seymour de Ricci; The Clarendon Press for 'Form and Matter in the Publication of Research' from *The Review of English Studies* by R. B. Mc-Kerrow, for 'Question and Answer' from *Autobiography* by R. G. Collingwood, for 'The Textual Criticism of English Classics' from *Portrait of a Scholar* by R. W. Chapman, and for 'The Rationale of Copy-Text' by W. W. Greg from *Collected Papers* edited by J. C. Maxwell; Rupert Hart-Davis Ltd for 'The Format of Books' from *ABC for Book-Collectors* by John Carter; The Historical Association for extracts from *Wanderings and Homes of Manuscripts* by M. R. James, to be reprinted in full by Messrs William Dawson & Sons on behalf of the Association; Modern Language Association of America for an extract from the Modern Language Association Style-Sheet.